W9-ATX-372

MICROWAVE
COOKBOOK

Good Cook's Library

MICROWAVE
COOKBOOK

Crescent Books
New York

© 1988 Ottenheimer Publishers, Inc.
This 1988 edition published by
Crescent Books, by arrangement with
Ottenheimer Publishers, Inc.,
distributed by Crown Publishers, Inc.,
225 Park Avenue South, New York, New York 10003

All rights reserved.

Printed and bound in Spain

ISBN 0-517-66212-4
h g f e d c b a

Contents

About this Book

Curiosity leads the experienced and inexperienced cook to try all new methods of cooking. Since the appearance of the first microwave ovens, cooks have been following their progress with increasing interest. Once a cook has had the pleasure of experimenting with a microwave, they come to the conclusion that it can be of great service to the household. There is no better way of cooking fish than with the microwave. Delicate fillets of fish are cooked to perfection in no time, remain succulent and do not fall to pieces. Complicated sauces are made easy and the results are delicate, creamy and delicious. Vegetables, meat and side dishes cooked in the microwave are superb.

This full-color picture cookbook for the microwave contains **204** tested recipes. Its comprehensive directions demonstrate how versatile this modern convenience is. Here you will find the best recipes, and each has been photographed exclusively for this volume. These brilliant pictures will inspire you to experiment. The uncomplicated recipes guarantee that everything tastes wonderful and is easy to prepare.

The practical chapter headings will help you with your choice of recipes. Soups and Sauces show you how quickly a delicious soup made with fresh ingredients can be put on the table; how easy it is to prepare sauces; and how simple it is to make attractive side dishes.

Fish lovers will be inspired by the suggestions in the chapter entitled Fish and Seafood. They prove that the microwave oven is ideal for the preparation of fish.

Of course, crisp roasts can only be prepared in a combination oven, i.e. one which has a grill, convection and conventional oven capabilities. Despite this, however, the simple microwave oven has advantages for Meat and Poultry dishes. It is excellent for stews, casseroles or roasts with gravy.

Vegetables taste wonderful when cooked in the microwave. Ratatouille, cooked to perfection, keeps the contrasting colors of peppers, tomatoes and zucchini. Creams and puddings take a long time to prepare using conventional methods, but they are particularly successful and effortless in the microwave. The recipes under the heading Desserts and Drinks are proof of this.

An important prerequisite for the best possible results is following the instructions exactly. If you follow the recipe directions you will find that cooking in a microwave is an enjoyable experience. A bleep announces each new cooking stage and you will soon enjoy using your microwave. If you have an oven with a stronger output than 500 or 600 watts, the conversion tables at the end of this book will help you to find the appropriate cooking times. Learning to use a microwave is the same as learning to use any conventional oven. Make yourself familiar with your microwave, preferably through experimenting with various recipes. At first, set the timer for less than the recommended time, then cook the food for a little longer, if necessary.

Since all theory is often dull and sometimes difficult to understand, this book has been produced with full color pictures. Instructions for the correct setting for the equipment, the most suitable dishes for cooking, thawing and heating, and helpful tips are in each recipe.

The exciting thing about a microwave is that it allows even novices to attempt more difficult dishes, and it is in this spirit that this book has been written. It is a culinary adventure. Working housewives with little spare time, people who cook for only one or two, and cooking enthusiasts who delight in trying new techniques with new equipment will find this cookbook most helpful.

Important Information

Before operating a microwave, become thoroughly familiar with it. Follow the maker's instructions carefully. Remember never to cook eggs in their shells and always to cook them at a defrost setting. The microwave should not be installed near other cooking sources, because heat and steam can damage it. The advice center at the electric company or a consumer organization in your town has additional information about microwave cooking.

Characteristics of Microwaves

In contrast with gas or electric ovens, which first heat the cooking container in order to warm the food in them, the microwave oven stays cold. Heat is generated in the food itself. An example of this process is if you have cold hands, you rub them together to make them warm. Microwaves work in exactly the same way when they heat up food. Microwaves are electro-magnetic waves, similar to radio and television waves. Microwaves are in constantly vibrating movement and are differentiated by the number of vibrations per second. When the high frequency microwaves come in contact with food or liquid they activate the minute food particles, or molecules, so that they move quickly against each other, causing friction. The molecules generate inconceivably fast vibrations and produce such high frictional heat that the food cooks. There is no detour past heat conduction as in a pan. The microwave cooking process spreads from the surface to the center of the food by conduction.

The deeper the microwaves penetrate a piece of meat, the less effective they are. The energy is halved after 1 inch. For this reason, some foods must be stirred or turned around or over. This is also the reason that flat and small portions cook so quickly in the microwaves. The larger the amount of food, the greater the consumption of time and energy. A useful rule of thumb: double measure, almost double time; half measure, half the time. According to this simple formula, especially with small portions, energy and time savings of up to 80% can be achieved.

As with any other new piece of equipment, it takes a certain amount of time to become thoroughly familiar with the operation of a microwave. After only a few weeks the microwave be-

comes indispensable. It cannot replace a conventional oven entirely, but it is an important addition to the kitchen.

The Correct Equipment

Glass, china, pottery, and plastic dishes are all suitable for use in microwave cooking. These materials do not act as a barrier to microwaves. Traditional metal cooking utensils, on the other hand, are not suitable; they reflect the microwaves. For the same reason, aluminum foil cannot be used for wrap cooking in the microwave. If you wish to cook a whole chicken, the sections that cook fastest (particularly the wings), can be covered after a few minutes with aluminum foil. This prevents them from cooking further and drying out. Be sure the foil does not touch the sides or top of the microwave.

Microwaves and Frozen Foods

These are ideal partners. In the microwave, frozen foods are gently defrosted and cooked in the shortest possible time. They retain the maximum flavor, smell, and nutritional value without becoming overcooked.

Food Preparation

Microwave cooking is also healthy cooking. The short cooking time preserves the heat-sensitive vitamins in the food better than conventional cooking methods. Also, all foods can be cooked in their own juice or with a minimum of water. As a result, vegetables taste especially fresh and natural. Strong seasonings, most of all salt, are unnecessary in microwave cooking. Excessive use of fats is not necessary. Additional tips are on page **10**.

Browning

Microwave ovens are excellent for heating, defrosting and cooking, but not for roasting and browning. To achieve browning, special browning dishes should be used. These are first warmed for a few minutes in the microwave and then the foods are placed in them.

Combination Microwave Ovens

There are some ovens in which microwaves are combined with heat from above or below or with convection heat and a grill. In these ovens, roasts and soufflés acquire an appetizing, crisp coating.

Did You Know...

Small Quantities— Large Quantities

Small portions cook much faster in a microwave than large ones. A simple rule of thumb: double quantity, almost double time; half quantity, half time.

Small Dishes in the Right Place

Several small dishes, such as dessert bowls, should be arranged in a circle in the microwave, leaving the center empty. Turn the dishes after half the cooking time.

Steaming

Steam can escape through poorly fitting lids. Prevent this by using a piece of wax paper or a paper towel placed between the dish and lid. The food will cook in its own steam, retaining flavor and moisture.

Deep and Shallow Dishes

The dishes in the picture each hold 1½ quarts, but food will take longer to cook in the deeper dish. The surface area of the food is greater in the shallow dish, allowing the microwaves to be more effective.

Brown "Roasting"

Some foods do not brown in solo microwaves. If you would like a crispy coating, use a browning dish. Place small pieces of meat in the pre-heated, greased dish, roast for a few minutes, turn, and cook the other side.

Browning Poultry

Poultry takes on an attractive brown color if it is coated before cooking with melted butter and mild paprika powder.

Microwave Recipes

Many delicious recipes can be easily adapted to microwave recipes. As a rule, only a third to half of the given liquid is necessary. For ingredients such as uncooked rice or dried beans, however, it is essential to use the full amount of liquid.

Use Less Fat

In many recipes it is possible to reduce the amount of fat. This also reduces calories. Small pats of butter or a little oil can be used to add flavor.

Minimize Temperature Differences

Because the middle of the oven receives less microwave energy, thorough stirring from the outside to the inside equalizes the temperature differences and shortens the cooking time.

Turning Souffles

When a recipe cannot be stirred or turned, such as a soufflé or a cake, the dish should be rotated once or twice during the cooking time.

Round Dishes

Foods cook more evenly in round dishes than in square or rectangular ones. More energy is concentrated in the corners of square or rectangular dishes, so the food overcooks in the corners.

Paper Towels as an Aid

With certain foods, it is an advantage if the steam can escape. Paper towels are particularly useful, as they prevent fat splatters and soak up overflowing liquids. They also help brown bacon slices.

Browning with Soy Sauce

Small pieces of meat that should be browned can also be brushed with soy sauce. In addition to the color, the meat acquires a distinctive Far Eastern flavor. Salt can be eliminated when soy sauce is used.

Meat Thermometer

This is a useful tool for microwave cooking, especially for large pieces of meat. Some ovens come equipped with a temperature probe. There are also thermometers available that are designed for microwaves. Metal meat thermometers should not be used.

Less Salt

Foods cooked in the microwave retain natural flavors. Seasonings such as salt should be used sparingly and only after cooking.

Popcorn

Special microwave popcorn can be made easily in the microwave. Put the paper bag containing the corn in the oven and cook at full power for 3½ minutes until it "pops". Special poppers are available, also.

Vegetables in the Microwave

Correct Cooking

The microwave is ideal for vegetables and potatoes. They retain flavor, color and texture cooking in their own juices or a little water. Minerals and vitamins are retained, because of the short cooking time and minimum use of liquids. Vegetables can be prepared more naturally in the microwave oven.

Fresh, water-retaining and low fiber vegetables such as tomatoes, cucumber, spinach or mushrooms, are delicious cooked in the microwave. They need only 1–2 tablespoons of water per 4 ounces of vegetables, and are cooked at full power. (The cooking time depends on the type of vegetable and the power capacity of the oven.)

Correct Preparation

Vegetables cooked in their own juices are full of flavor. It is important, however, that sufficient steam can develop in the dish. Only light seasoning is required to enhance natural flavor. Minerals are particularly well retained by careful cooking in the microwave. For this reason, salt lightly and, preferably, season with fresh herbs.

The vegetables should always be cooked in a closed container, so that no liquid is lost and nothing dries out. For best results, use dishes with close-fitting lids. Plastic wrap is also suitable.

Cutting Vegetables

Prepare the vegetables for cooking in the microwave in the usual way. Wash thoroughly, then trim and cut according to the recipe, either cubing or slicing. As the cooking time is also dependent on the size of the pieces, cut the vegetables as small as possible if they should be cooked quickly.

It is important to cut the vegetables the same size and thickness so that the vegetables are evenly cooked. Carrots and potatoes should be cut either in very thin slices or very fine cubes if possible, with a food processor.

Cooking Whole Vegetables

Whole vegetables such as cauliflower or potatoes need a longer cooking time, as the microwaves lose energy the deeper they penetrate. A few technical hints will help you to achieve even cooking.

Whole vegetables with fixed skins, such as peppers, potatoes, egg plant or tomatoes, should be pricked a few times with a fork before cooking. The steam can then escape without bursting the skin.

Fiber-rich vegetables, such as carrots, brussels sprouts, potatoes, beans, peas or cabbage require slightly more liquid for cooking and need a slightly longer cooking time than water-retaining vegetables. The bottom of the cooking dish for these vegetables should be completely covered with liquid.

Instead of cooking vegetables with water, they can also be steamed in butter or margarine. Place the prepared vegetables and butter in the dish at the same time. The advantage over stove-top cooking is that less butter is required. The vegetables are more wholesome and contain fewer calories.

Either salt the vegetables after cooking, or dissolve the salt in the cooking liquid. If it is added directly to the vegetables, dry areas develop, as salt absorbs moisture from the vegetables.

Canned or preserved vegetables are pre-cooked and need only to be re-heated in the microwave. Place the vegetables in a shallow dish with 1–2 tablespoons of liquid, fresh herbs and a little butter. Cover the dish with a lid or plastic wrap. Stir once or twice while cooking.

With unevenly shaped vegetables such as broccoli, the tender florets cook more quickly than the stalks. Therefore, arrange them in a single layer on a round dish with the florets toward the middle and the stalks toward the outside.

Finely chopped vegetables should be stirred once or twice during cooking, and always from the inside to the outside. This distributes the heat evenly.

Whole or halved vegetables such as stuffed tomatoes or artichokes should be arranged in a circle in a shallow dish. Leave at least 1 inch between the vegetables. The middle of the dish should be empty. During the cooking, turn the dish as well as the vegetables.

If you leave the cooked whole vegetables to stand for a short time before serving, the heat is more evenly distributed. The heat penetrates from the outside to the inside, so that the inside also becomes soft without overcooking the outside.

Meat and Fish in the Microwave

Large Roasts

Tender cuts of veal, pork, lamb or game cook extremely well in the microwave. Ground beef also can be prepared in many ways. Smaller pieces of meat under 1 pound cook so quickly, that they do not brown successfully. Larger pieces of meat need a longer cooking time, so they browning slightly. The cooking time per 1 pound of meat is 10–12 minutes at full power.

Fatter roasts of over 1 pound should be placed on an upturned saucer in a shallow dish. The meat juices collect in the dish and the meat does not cook in its own juices. Place the meat down on either the fatter or larger side at first, and turn over after half the cooking time.

Smaller Cuts of Meat

Smaller cuts are prepared the same as larger ones. Rinse briefly, dry with paper towels and season. Salt sparingly. Use a browning dish for quick-roasting pieces for crispness. For stews, smaller pieces of meat do not need to be seared.

When using irregularly shaped pieces of meat, such as chicken thighs or legs, the thinner parts cook more quickly. Cover these thinner parts with foil before cooking. The foil should not touch the inside of the oven. There should be at least 1 inch gap between the foil and the oven lining.

Fish and Fish Filets

Fish prepared in the microwave oven is a delicacy. Its characteristic flavor is particularly well preserved, as only the minimum of liquid is required, or sometimes none at all. With most recipes, it is recommended to let the fish stand for a few minutes after turning off the oven. The heat is evenly distributed as a result of this post-cooking time. The fish does not overcook and remains tender and juicy.

Bluefish needs very little liquid for cooking. Concentrated stock ¼ inch deep in the dish is enough. Before putting in the microwave, sprinkle the fish with lemon juice and take care not to damage the skin, as this affects the blue color.

Whole Fish and Mussels

Whole fish and mussels can be successfully prepared in the microwave. As a rule, fish dishes are cooked at full power. Whole fish weighing more than 2 pounds are first cooked at the highest cooking cycle, then finished at less power. All dishes should be sparingly salted, so that the delicate flavor of the fish remains.

Large whole fish are cooked in an open dish with only a little liquid and turned over once during the cooking time. The fish stays very moist if it is covered with slices of bacon. At the beginning, cover the thinner tail with aluminum foil.

Larger roasts are usually cooked in an open dish. For a brown roast, use a browning dish or sear the meat on the stove top and finish cooking in the microwave. This also saves time. In a combination oven, the meat becomes crisp and brown.

Let the roast stand for 10 minutes after cooking, either in the microwave or outside it. Cover the dish with foil. The roast remains tender and juicy, the juices distribute themselves through the meat, and the temperature becomes even.

Smaller pieces of meat, such as chops and medallions, cook best with a spicy sauce, such as tomato sauce. The meat remains tender and juicy and the sauce adds color.

Smaller cuts of meat, which have a short cooking time need additional color. Add tomato purée, red wine or onion skins, which enhance flavor and add color.

Irregularly shaped pieces of fish, such as salmon cutlets, should be placed with the thinner parts to the middle. Thicker parts require a longer cooking time and receive more energy at the outside of the dish.

Fish fillets should be cooked in a closed dish with a little butter or liquid. Cover the dish with a lid or with plastic wrap.

If you need to cook more than one whole fish at a time, put them in a circular glass dish. The tails should be placed side by side, so that the thickness is the same throughout. The underside should face out. After half the cooking time, turn the fish so that the back is facing out.

Mussels must be undamaged and closed, and the beard removed. Cook in a glass-covered dish. Completely immerse the mussels in liquid and seasonings. Scampi should be placed in a suitable buttered dish without the under-shell and with the back shell facing down. Cook in an open dish.

Power Chart For All Appliances

The differences between 650 and 720 watts in defrosting, reheating and cooking time is negligible. Allow just a little more time in cooking with the 650 watt appliance.

Power Chart For All Appliances

500 Watt	600 Watt	700 Watt
(45 seconds)	(30 seconds)	(30 seconds)
1¼ minutes	1 minute	1 minute
1¾ minutes	1½ minutes	1¼ minutes
2½ minutes	2 minutes	1¾ minutes
2¾ minutes	2¼ minutes	2 minutes
3 minutes	2½ minutes	2 minutes
3½ minutes	3 minutes	2½ minutes
4½ minutes	4 minutes	3½ minutes
5½ minutes	5 minutes	4¼ minutes
6½ minutes	6 minutes	5 minutes
8 minutes	7 minutes	6 minutes
9 minutes	8 minutes	7 minutes
10½ minutes	9 minutes	7½ minutes
11½ minutes	10 minutes	8½ minutes
12½ minutes	11 minutes	9½ minutes
13½ minutes	12 minutes	10 minutes
15 minutes	13 minutes	11 minutes
16 minutes	14 minutes	12 minutes
17 minutes	15 minutes	13 minutes
23 minutes	20 minutes	17 minutes
28 minutes	25 minutes	21 minutes
34 minutes	30 minutes	26 minutes
39 minutes	35 minutes	30 minutes
45 minutes	40 minutes	34 minutes
56 minutes	50 minutes	43 minutes

Reheating Food in the Microwave

The time required to reheat food depends upon the power of the microwave: 500, 600, or 700 watts. If the weight of food is doubled then, the reheating time is also doubled.

Food	Measure	Time	Further Instructions
Potatoes	1⅓ cups	2–3 minutes	Add a little water and cover.
Rice	1½ cups		
Noodles	3 cups		
Fish Filets	1 pound	2½–3½ minutes	Add a little water and cover.
Roast meat in sauce or gravy	1 pound	4–6 minutes	When hot, cover, turning often.
Poultry	½ chicken	4–5 minutes	Add a little water.
Coffee or tea	⅔ cup	1–1¾ minutes	
Water or mulled wine	⅔ cup	1–2 minutes	Stir.
Milk or cocoa	⅔ cup	½–1	Stir.
Clear soup	1 cup	2–2½ minutes	Cover and stir.
Thick soup	1 cup	2–3	Cover and stir.
Plate Meals	1 portion	2–3	Cover and add water if dry.

Defrosting Frozen Food

This chart is for defrosting frozen food, but not reheating. Approximate time is given for low setting. The rule is double the weight, double the time, half the weight half the time.

Food	Measure	Time		Further Instructions
Fish				
Whole	1 pound	9–12	minutes	Shield tail and fins with foil and cover; turn, let stand for 10 minutes.
Filet	½ pound	5–7	minutes	Cover, turn once.
Scampi	½ pound	7–8	minutes	Cover, turn once.
Mussels	½ pound	5	minutes	Turn once.
Meat and Sausages				
Roasts	1 pound	12–15	minutes	Turn once, let stand for 15 minutes.
Cutlets	½ pound	4–5	minutes	Cover, turn once.
Ground meat	½ pound	10	minutes	Cover, break up the meat after 5 minutes, let stand 10 minutes.
Sausages, Bacon Ham	½ pound	4–6	minutes	Cover.
Desserts and Bread				
Puff pastry (uncooked)	1¼ cups	2–3	minutes	Place on paper towels, turn once, let stand for 5 minutes.
Sponge cake	1 piece	½–1½	minutes	Place on paper towels, let stand for 5 minutes.
Fruit pie	1 piece	2–4	minutes	Place on paper towels, let stand for 5 minutes.
Tarts	1 piece	½–1½	minutes	Thaw, let stand for 10 minutes.
Bread	1 slice	½–1	minutes	Place on paper towels.
Rolls	1 piece	½–1½	minutes	Place on paper towels.
Poultry and Game				
Chicken	2 pounds	20–30	minutes	Shield wing tips and drum sticks with foil, cover, let stand for 10–15 minutes.
Chicken breast	½ pound	8–10	minutes	Turn once, let stand for 5 minutes.
Drumsticks	½ pound	8–10	minutes	Cover, let stand for 5 minutes.
Duck	4½ pounds	35–50	minutes	Turn twice, the 2nd time cover drumsticks with foil.
Goose	6 pounds	50–65	minutes	Turn 3 times, 2nd time cover wings and drumsticks with foil, let stand for 40–45 minutes.
Game	2 pounds	20–35	minutes	Turn once.
Vegetables				
Broccoli (raw)	1 cup	5–7	minutes	Turn once, separate, let stand for 5 minutes.
Spinach (raw)	2½ cups	3–5	minutes	Turn once, separate, let stand for 5 minutes.
Peas (raw)	1½ cups	4–5	minutes	Stir once.
Dairy Products				
Cream	1 cup	3–5	minutes	Remove lid, thaw only, let stand 5 minutes.
Butter	1 cup	4–6	minutes	Remove any foil, let stand for 10–20 minutes.
Cottage Cheese	1 cup	5–7	minutes	Remove any foil, let stand for 10 minutes.
Cheese	1 cup	1–2	minutes	Thaw only, let stand for 10 minutes.
Fruit				
Soft fruit	1 cup	4–6	minutes	Arrange flat, stir carefully, let stand for 5 minutes.
Stoned fruit	1 cup	5–7	minutes	Arrange flat, cover.
Stock				
Meat, poultry, vegetable	1 cup	9–11	minutes	Cover.

Appetizers

There are many dishes in this chapter which can be prepared in a few moments, for those occasions when time is short or you are not too hungry.

Perhaps you would like to offer guests something to eat. The microwave oven is particularly useful when you need to use ingredients out of the store cupboard to make small snacks, such as bread, tomatoes, eggs, ham or sausage. They are quickly made, taste good and look attractive, as the toast in the picture shows.

In addition, this chapter contains some impressive dishes, such as the chicken mousseline which is suitable as a starter to a fine dinner or as part of a cold buffet table. These recipes use a minimum of ingredients which are easily available and which need only a few techniques. Attractively garnished, these dishes are a pleasure to the eye.

Bacon Fingers

Very quick

110 calories per finger
Preparation time: 15 minutes
Cooking time: 2½ (3) minutes
Yield: 20 fingers

---
4 oz. frozen puff pastry

Flour for pastry board
---
20 thin slices lean bacon

Defrost the pastry. Sprinkle a thin layer of flour on the work surface and roll out pastry to a thickness of 1/16 in. Then cut it in strips measuring ½ in. wide and 5 in. long. Wrap the bacon slices in spirals round the pastry strips. • Put a paper towel on a plate and cook half the fingers on this for 2½ (3) minutes at 600 (500) watts. Repeat with the remainder of the fingers.

Tip: the pastry strips will be easier to handle if placed in the freezer for 10 minutes.

Sesame Fingers

Very easy

18 calories per finger
Preparation time: 15 minutes
Yield: 20 fingers

---
4 oz. frozen puff pastry

Flour for pastry board
---
1 egg white

Salt
---
1 tbs. sesame seeds

Defrost the pastry. Sprinkle a thin layer of flour on the work surface and roll out pastry to a thickness of 1/16 in. in a rectangle measuring 6 × 10 in. Whisk the egg white with a pinch of salt and brush the pastry with it. Using a pastry wheel, cut out 20 fingers measuring ¼ × 2½ in. Sprinkle the sesame seeds over the fingers and form them into spirals. Put half the fingers on a shallow dish and cover with a paper towel. Cook for 2¼ (2¾) minutes at 600 (500) watts. Repeat with the remainder of the fingers.

Toast with Ham and Cheese

Particularly easy; good value

310 calories per serving
Preparation time: 15 minutes
Cooking time: 1 minute

Serves: 2 people

2 slices of toasting bread
1 tsp. mustard
2 slices ham, each weighing 1 oz.
1 tomato
2 sage leaves
½ cup semi-soft cheese, e.g. Gruyère
Pepper

Toast the bread on both sides. Spread one side with the mustard and put one slice of ham on each. Wash the tomato, remove the stalk, slice and arrange on top of the ham. Put a sage leaf on each piece of toast.

Cut the cheese in ⅛ in. thick slices and lay on the toast. Sprinkle with pepper. • Cook for 1 minute at 490 (500) watts until the cheese has melted.

Variations: You can also prepare the toast without the sage leaves, using instead a peach half or a pear half cut in a fan shape and laid on top of the cheese. Cook the cheese until melted as described above. Alternatively, you can omit the mustard and ham, instead spreading the toast slices with chopped anchovy filets. Alternatively, use ¼ cup mushrooms, trimmed and finely sliced.

Chicken Livers with Apple

More difficult; good value

420 calories per serving
Preparation time: 30 minutes
Cooking time: 9¼ (10¾) minutes

Serves: 2 people

2 apples
1 small onion
6 oz. chicken livers
4 slices French bread
2 tsp. butter
Salt, pepper
Pinch dried thyme
1 tbs. cider

Peel and core the apples. Cut into 4 rings approximately ¼ in. thick. Coarsely grate the remainder of the apples. Peel and grate the onion. Trim and finely slice the livers. Heat a browning dish for 4 (4½) min-

utes at 600 (500) watts. Toast the slices of bread and put on two plates. Melt half the butter in the heated dish, add the livers and cook for 1 (1¼) minutes at 600 (500) watts. • Turn the chicken livers and finish cooking for 1 (1¼) minutes at 600 (500) watts. Take the livers out of the dish. Sprinkle them with salt, pepper and thyme. Put the rest of the butter in the dish. Put the grated apple and the onion on one half of the dish and the apple rings on the other half. Cook them all for 3 (3½) minutes at 600 (500) watts. • Remove the apple slices. Mix the livers with the grated apple and the onion. Share between the plates. Mix the cooking juices with the cider and add this and the apple slices to the plates. Heat the bread and the livers for ¼ minute at 600 (500) watts.

Mushrooms on Toast

Very easy

230 calories per serving
Preparation time: 10 minutes
Cooking time: 6 (6¾) minutes

Serves: 4 people

1 shallot
1 tbs. butter
¾ cup mushrooms
1 tbs. white wine
Salt, pepper
2 tsp. cornflour
½ cup cram
4 slices toasting bread
2 tsp. brandy
1 tsp. finely chopped chives

Peel and finely chop the shallot and stew in the butter for 1 (1¼) minutes at 600 (500) watts. Wash the mushrooms and quarter them (slice larger mushrooms). Add to the shallot with the white wine. Season with salt and pepper and cook, covered, for 2 (2½) minutes at 600 (500) watts. Whip the cornflour with the cream, add to the mushrooms and cook everything for an additional 3 minutes at 490 (500) watts. Meanwhile toast the bread. Add the brandy to the mushrooms and adjust the seasoning. Divide between the toast slices and serve immediately, sprinkled with the chopped chives.

Variations: you can also prepare the toast with dried mushrooms, or morels. Or chanterelles mixed with mushrooms can be used. In addition, the bread can be covered with a slice of ham, warmed for ½ minute at 490 (500) watts, before adding the mushroom sauce to the toast.

Chicken on Toast

Very quick

210 calories per serving
Preparation time: 15 minutes
Cooking time: 2½ (2¾) minutes

Serves: 4 people

1 tsp. mustard
2 tbs. Philadelphia cream cheese
1 tbs. cream
Salt, pepper
Pinch sugar
2 boneless chicken breasts
4 slices white bread
1 tsp. butter
½ small cucumber
Paprika

Whip the mustard with the cheese and the cream. Season with salt, pepper and sugar. Lay the chicken breasts in a dish and cook, covered, for 2½ (2¾) minutes at 360 (330) watts. • Meanwhile, toast the bread, spread with butter. Wash the cucumber, cut in slices, sprinkle with salt and pepper and cover the slices of toast with it. Skin the chicken breasts, cut diagonally in slices, and arrange on the cucumber slices. Put the cheese in a piping bag fitted with a star-shaped nozzle and decorate the chicken slices. Sprinkle with paprika.

Tip: Serve the chicken lukewarm. You can also use cooked chicken left-overs, in which case warm up the finely chopped meat with 1 tbs. white wine or chicken stock, cover, and cook for ½ minute at 490 (500) watts. The cheese can also be flavored with watercress or herbs.

Cheese Tartlets

Good value for money

520 calories per serving
Preparation time: 15 minutes
Resting time: 1-2 hours
Cooking time: 10½ (11¼) minutes
Serves: 2 people

Pastry:
¼ cup flour
2 tbs. butter
2 tbs. ice-cold water
Pinch salt
Filling:
1 tsp. butter
1 egg
Freshly grated cheese, Gruyère
1 cup cream
Salt and pepper
Grated nutmeg
Pinch paprika

Sieve the flour on to a board. Cut the butter into small pieces and add to flour. Rub the flour and butter between your fingers until it resembles breadcrumbs. Make a hollow in the middle, add the water and the salt, and working from the middle, quickly mix to a dough. Leave the pastry to rest in a cool place for 1-2 hours. Lightly grease 3 in. tartlet dishes with the butter. Roll out the pastry to a thickness of ¼ in. Line the dishes with the pastry, pressing it down well. Prick with a fork, so that it does not bubble up. Line each dish with paper and fill with dried beans. Bake tartlet blind for 3 (3½) minutes at 600 (500) watts. Remove the paper and beans and bake the pastry again for 2 (2½) minutes at 600 (500) watts. • Mix the egg, cheese and cream. Season with salt, pepper and nutmeg. Divide the filling equally between the tartlets.

Cook for 5 (5¼) minutes at 180 (150) watts until set. Sprinkle with a small amount of paprika and serve lukewarm.

Tip: Do not fill the pastry cases until just before putting them in the oven, so that they do not become soggy. When making tartlets for 4 people, put them on a small baking tray. Bake the pastry for 3 (3½) minutes at 600 (500) watts after baking blind and increase the final stage of the cooking by 2 minutes. Tartlets cooked in advance can be warmed up for ½ (¾) minute at 600 (500) watts.

Cheese Pudding

200 calories per serving
Preparation time: 15 minutes
Cooking time: 4 (4¼) minutes
Serves: 4 people

3 tbs. cream
2 egg yolks
½ cup Gruyère
1 tbs. flour
2 egg whites
Salt, pepper, grated nutmeg
1 tbs. butter

Whip the cream lightly. Beat the egg yolks and mix with cream. Finely grate the cheese, and add with the sieved flour to the egg mixture. Whisk the egg whites until stiff and fold into cheese mixture. Season with salt, pepper and nutmeg. Grease two 9 in. soufflé dishes with the butter. Fill the dishes ¾ full with the cheese mixture. Cook the cheese snacks for 1 minute at 490 (500) watts and finally for 3 (3¼) minutes at 360 (330) watts.

Stuffed Avocados

More difficult
More expensive

430 calories per serving
Preparation time: 15 minutes
Cooking time: 2½ (2¾) minutes

Serves: 4 people

2 avocados
Juice of ½ lemon
Salt, pepper
3 tbs. cream
2 boned chicken breasts

Cut the avocados in half lengthwise and take out the pit. Using a melon baller, make 20 small balls. Carefully remove the rest of the avocado flesh from the skin, mash with a fork and mix immediately with some lemon juice. Also sprinkle the avocado balls with lemon juice. Season both with salt and pepper and mix the mashed avocado with the cream. • Season the chicken breasts with salt and pepper and cook, covered, in a dish for 2½ (2¾) minutes at 360 (330) watts. Cut the meat in strips and mix with the mashed avocado. Put this mixture into the avocado skins and garnish each with 5 avocado balls.

Toast with Avocado

Very easy

400 calories per serving
Preparation time: 10 minutes
Cooking time: 9 (10½) minutes

Serves: 2 people

2 slices toasting bread
1 tsp. butter
1 ripe avocado
Salt, pepper
2 tsp. cream cheese
1 tsp. Gruyère cheese, freshly grated
1 tsp. freshly chopped chervil

Heat a browning dish for 3 (3½) minutes at 600 (500) watts. Melt the butter in the dish, add the slices of bread and coat well with the butter. Bake the bread for 1 (1¼) minutes at 600 (500) on each side. Peel, halve and pit the avocado. Lay each half, cut side down, on a slice of bread. Cut the rounded side at intervals of about ¼ in., diagonally. Season with salt and pepper, top with the cream cheese and cover with the Gruyère. • Cook the avocado for 4 (4½) minutes at 600 (500) watts. Sprinkle with the chervil and serve.

Cheese Omelette

Very quick

290 calories per serving
Preparation time: 10 minutes
Cooking time: 6 (6¾) minutes

Serves: 2 people

3 egg yolks
2 level tbs. Emmental or Parmesan, freshly grated
3 tbs. milk
Salt, pepper
3 egg whites
1 tbs. butter

Beat the egg yolks with the cheese and milk. Season with salt and pepper. Beat the egg whites with a pinch of salt until stiff and fold into the egg yolks. Grease a large dish with the butter and heat for 1 (1¼) minutes at 600 (500) watts. • Pour in the beaten mixture and cook for 3 (3¼) minutes at 360 (330) watts. Loosen the edges and cook for another 2 (2¼) minutes at 360 (330) watts. Fold the omelette carefully with a rubber spatula and serve.

Cheese Slices with Ham

Economical

500 calories per serving
Preparation time: 15 minutes

Serves: 2 people

1 shallot
2 tbs. butter
4 mushrooms
3 tbs. white wine
6 tbs. cream
Salt, pepper, grated nutmeg
Pinch paprika
1 tsp. butter
2 slices toasting bread
2 small slices ham
½ cup Gruyère cheese, freshly grated
2 eggs

Peel and finely chop the shallot and put in a dish with the butter. Wash and dry the mushrooms, cut in slices and add to the dish. Cook for 2 (2½) minutes at 600 (500) watts. Add the wine, then the cream and cook for 2 (2½) minutes at 600 (500) watts. Season the sauce with salt, pepper, nutmeg and paprika. Grease a dish with the butter. Cook the bread slices on both sides for 2 (2½) minutes at 600 (500) watts on each side. Lay the ham slices on the bread. Mix the cheese with the shallot and the mushrooms and divide between the slices. Cook for 4 (4½) minutes at 600 (500) watts. Heat a browning dish for 3 (3½) minutes at 600 (500) watts. Break the eggs into this and cook for 1 minute at 490 (500) watts. Then take them out of the oven and leave covered for 1 minute. Serve the fried eggs on top of the cheese slices.

Cheese Slices with Green Peppercorns

Very Quick

310 calories per serving
Preparation time: 5 minutes
Cooking time: 7 (8½) minutes

Serves: 2 people

1 tbs. butter
2 slices toasting bread
3 tbs. white wine
1 tsp. green peppercorns in brine
½ cup Gruyère cheese, freshly grated
1 egg
½ clove garlic
Salt, pepper, grated nutmeg

Heat a browning dish for 2 (2½) minutes at 600 (500) watts. Let the butter melt on this. Lay the bread slices in the butter and cook for 1 (1¼) minutes at 600 (500) watts on each side. Moisten the bread with a dash of the wine. Put the green peppercorns in a small sieve and rinse with cold water. Mix the cheese with the egg. Peel the garlic and press or crush. Mix the remainder of the wine, the green peppercorns and the garlic with the cheese and egg. Season with salt, pepper and nutmeg. Divide the cheese mixture between the bread slices and cook for 3 (3½) minutes at 600 (500) watts.

Tip: If you have a combination microwave oven with grill, the cheese slices can be browned further under the grill.

Variations: The toast slices can also be covered with slices of ham. The green peppercorns can be replaced by herbs or diced red peppers. Before serving, the slices can be garnished with paprika.

Chicken Mousseline

More difficult

170 calories per serving
Preparation time: 40 minutes
Cooking time: 6 (6½) minutes
Serves: 6 people

| 1 cup cream |
| 9 oz. boned and skinned chicken breasts |
| Salt |
| 1 tsp. grated lemon rind |
| White pepper |
| Grated nutmeg |
| Pinch ground coriander |

Pour the cream into a bowl and put it into the freezer for about 20 minutes. Cut the meat into cubes, spread out on a plate and put this, too, into the freezer. Cut the half-frozen cream in pieces and liquidize in a food processor with the meat and a pinch of salt until a smooth purée is formed. Mix in the lemon rind and season with salt, pepper and nutmeg and coriander. Lay a piece of cling-film measuring about 16 × 20 in. on the table and spoon the mixture lengthwise down the cling-film. Roll up the film and form the mixture into a sausage shape. Secure the ends. The roll should measure about 2 in. in diameter and 6 in. long. Make the roll airtight by securing each end with kitchen string. Put the roll in a dish containing about ¼ cup water in the middle of the microwave oven. Cook for 6 (6½) minutes at 360 (330) watts. Take out the chicken mousseline and leave to cool completely, wrapped in aluminum foil. Take off both wrappings, cut the cream in slices and serve with salad.

Variations: A fish mousseline can be prepared in the same way. In this case, do not use the lemon rind and replace the coriander with dill. Fish mousseline can be served warm with a sauce. For best results warm the slices before serving for 1 (1¼) minutes at 180 (150) watts.

Corn Salad with Bacon

Very Easy

430 calories per serving
Preparation time: 20 minutes
Cooking time: 7 (8¼) minutes

Serves: 4 people

| 4 slices white bread, crusts removed |
| ½ cup lambs lettuce |
| 3 tbs. white wine vinegar or sherry vinegar |
| 1 tbs. sharp mustard |
| Salt, pepper |
| 1 clove garlic |
| 6 tbs. walnut oil |
| 2 tbs. clarified butter |
| 2 oz. lean bacon |

Cut the bread into very small cubes. Wash and dry the lettuce. Mix the vinegar with the mustard and a little salt and pepper. Peel the garlic, press it and gradually mix it with the oil. Put the clarified butter in a bowl and warm for 1 (1¼) minutes at 600 (500) watts. Mix in the diced bread. Cook for 2 (2½) minutes at 600 (500) watts. Cut the bacon into small squares, place in a second bowl and bake until crisp for 4 (4½) minutes at 600 (500) watts. Toss the lettuce in a bowl with the dressing. Arrange on plates and sprinkle with the diced bread and bacon squares.

Gypsy Kebabs

Very Easy

690 calories per serving
Preparation time: 30 minutes
Cooking time: 12 (13¾) minutes

Serves: 2 people

1 onion
1 small zucchini
2 thin slices smoked bacon
¼ lb. rump steak
¼ lb. veal
2 frying sausages
Salt, pepper
Pinch paprika
1 tsp. oil
1 onion
3 tomatoes
1 tsp. butter
3 tsp. corn (canned)
1 tsp. tomato purée
4 tsp. cream
Cayenne pepper

Peel the onion, trim and wash the zucchini. Cut both into approximately ½ in. thick slices. Fold the bacon slices into squares. Cut the meat into 1–1½ in. cubes. Thread them all with the sausage on wooden skewers. Season with salt, pepper and paprika and sprinkle with oil. • For the sauce, peel the onion and chop it. Pour boiling water over the tomatoes, rinse them with cold water, skin, core and chop into cubes. Heat a browning dish for 4 (4½) minutes at 600 (500) watts. Put in the kebabs and cook on each side for 1 (1¼) minutes at 600 (500) watts on each side. Cover the kebabs with aluminum foil and leave to stand. Steam the onion with the butter in a dish for 1 (1¼) minutes at 600 (500) watts. Add the tomatoes and the drained corn to this and steam for 3 minutes at 490 (500) watts. Mix in the tomato purée and the

cream and season the sauce well with salt, pepper and some cayenne pepper. Finish cooking for 2 (2½) minutes at 360 (330) watts.

Pizza Toast

Very easy, good value

430 calories per serving
Preparation time: 20 minutes
Cooking time: 8 (9½) minutes

Serves: 2 people

1 tbs. olive oil
2 slices toasting bread
1 clove garlic
1 slice ham
4 slices salami
4 olives
1 tomato
3 anchovies
1 mushroom
Salt, pepper
1 tsp. freshly chopped oregano
2 slices mozarella cheese

Heat a browning dish for 2 (2½) minutes at 600 (500) watts. Pour in the olive oil, add the bread slices and cook on both sides for 1 (1¼) minutes at 600 (500) watts on each side. Peel the garlic, press or crush and spread on the bread slices. Cut the ham in thin strips, quarter the salami slices. Halve the olives and pit them. Skin the tomato, core and chop finely. Coarsely chop the anchovies. Wipe the mushroom and slice finely. Spread all the ingredients on the bread and sprinkle with salt, pepper and oregano. Lay the slices of mozarella on top. Season again with salt and pepper and cook for 4 (4½) minutes at 600 (500) watts.

Pasta with Eggplant

More difficult

760 calories per serving
Preparation time: 40 minutes
Cooking time: 29 (32½) minutes

Serves: 3 people

1 medium-sized eggplant
Salt
1 large onion
1 clove garlic
2 tbs. olive oil
¾ cup egg noodles
4 ripe tomatoes
¾ cup mozarella cheese
1 tbs. butter
Pepper
4 basil leaves
2 tbs. Gruyère cheese, freshly grated

Wash and trim the eggplant and cut in ¼ in. thick slices. Sprinkle with salt and leave for 30 minutes. Then dry with kitchen paper. Peel the onion and chop finely. Peel and press the garlic. Heat a browning dish for 3 (3½) minutes at 600 (500) watts. Add some of the olive oil. Add the eggplant slices. Cook for 2 (2½) minutes at 600 (500) watts on each side. Put 3 cups salted water in a large glass dish. Cover and cook for 6 (6½) minutes at 600 (500) watts. Add the pasta, cover, and cook for 6 (6½) minutes at 600 (500) watts, then drain. Skin the tomatoes, onion, garlic and the remainder of the olive oil in a dish and cook for 5 (5½) minutes at 600 (500). Cut the mozarella in thin slices. Grease a dish with some of the butter. Layer the pasta with the eggplant, the tomatoes, the mozarella, a little salt and pepper and the coarsely chopped basil. Top with the grated cheese and the remainder of the butter and cook for 5 (5½) minutes at 600 (500) watts.

Whisked Omelette

Very Quick

210 calories per serving
Preparation time: 10 minutes
Cooking time: 5 minutes, 40 seconds (6 minutes, 20 seconds)

Serves: 2 people

3 egg yolks
2 tbs. cream
Salt, pepper
3 egg whites
1 tbs. butter

Beat the egg yolks with the cream and season with salt and pepper. Beat the egg whites with a pinch of salt until stiff. Fold the egg whites carefully into the egg yolks. Put the butter into a large, shallow glass dish and melt for 40 (50) seconds at 600 (500) watts. Add the egg mixture and cook for 3 (3¼) minutes at 360 (330) watts. Loosen the

edges of the egg mixture with a spatula and finish cooking for 2 (2½) minutes at 360 (330) watts. Fold the omelette carefully with a rubber spatula and place on a warmed plate.

Tip: The omelette is more successful if the egg white is whipped with a hand whisk. The omelette can be eaten with a variety of fillings, in which case it is presented differently. For instance, a vegetable filling should be prepared before the omelette is cooked. Melt some butter in a glass dish for 1 (1¼) minutes at 600 (500) watts. Add the vegetables and cook, covered, for 2 minutes or perhaps a little longer at 490 (500) watts. For omelette itself, put the butter in a dish, add the egg mixture and cook for 3 (3¼) minutes at 360 (330) watts. Then add the filling and finish the omelette as described above.

Macaroni with Ham and Spinach

Very easy

550 calories per serving
Preparation time: 15 minutes
Cooking time: 23 (25) minutes

Serves: 2 people

Salt
1¼ cups small macaroni shells
¼ lb. smoked ham
1 cup spinach
1 tbs. butter
1 hard-boiled egg
½ cup cream
Pepper
Nutmeg
1 tsp. each, freshly chopped marjoram and thyme
2 tbs. Emmental cheese, freshly grated

Put 3 cups water in a dish. Add a pinch of salt and

bring to a boil for 6 (6½) minutes at 600 (500) watts. Add the macaroni, cover, and cook for 8 (9) minutes at 600 (500) watts. Meanwhile, cut the ham in small squares. Drain the macaroni and mix with the ham. Trim and wash the spinach. Cook it for 3 minutes at 490 (500) watts with 1 tbs. water. Press out the water thoroughly, and cut in strips. Add this to the macaroni. Grease a suitable dish with the butter. Fill with the macaroni. Shell the egg, chop it finely and mix with the cream. Add salt, pepper, nutmeg and half of the herbs. Pour the egg mixture over the macaroni. Sprinkle the cheese over the top and cook for 6 (6½) minutes at 600 (500) watts. Sprinkle on the remainder of the herbs and serve.

Tip: You can halve the ingredients and serve this dish as a light meal.

Poached Eggs

Particularly fast

120 calories
Preparation time: 1 minute
Cooking time: 1½ (2¼) minutes

Serves: 1 egg

2 tbs. water
¼ tsp. vinegar
1 egg
1 tsp. butter
Salt, pepper
1 tsp. parsley, freshly chopped

Put the water and vinegar in a small dish or shallow soup bowl. Boil, covered, for ½ (¾) minute at 600 (500) watts. Crack open the egg, add to the dish, cover and poach for ½ (¾) minute at 360 (330) watts. Take the dish out of the oven and leave the egg in the liquid for 2 minutes without removing the lid. Then take out the egg and dry on kitchen paper. Put the butter in a small dish and melt for ½ (¾) minute at 600 (500) watts. Season with salt and pepper and parsley and pour over the egg.

Tip: If preparing 2 eggs, increase the cooking time of both the vinegar and water and the eggs by ½ minute each; for 3 eggs, increase 1 minute each. For best results, do not prepare more than 3 eggs at the same time. If cooking 3 eggs, change the position of the dish once or twice, so that the eggs will be evenly cooked.

Variation: Cook 1 tsp. chopped shallot with 1 tsp. butter in a covered dish for 1 (1¼) minutes at 600 (500) watts. Add 1¼ cups washed and chopped spinach, season with salt, pepper and nutmeg and cook, covered, for 3 (3½) minutes at 600 (500) watts. One half minute before the end of the cooking time, mix 3 tbs. cream with the spinach and add to the eggs before serving.

Variation: Cook 3 tbs. chicken stock with 1 cup cream for 3 (3½) minutes at 600 (500) watts until thick and reduced. Add 1 tsp. lemon juice, ½–1 tbs. capers and 1 oz. pickled ox tongue, cut in strips, to the sauce. Season with salt and pepper and add to the eggs before serving.

Fried Eggs

Very easy

120 calories
Preparation time: 5 minutes
Cooking time: 1 minute

Serves: 1 egg

1 tsp. butter
Salt, pepper
1 egg

Grease a shallow dish with the butter. Sprinkle with salt and pepper. Break the egg on to this. Cook for 1 minute at 490 (500) watts. Season with a little salt and pepper.

Tip: Only cook one egg at a time, so that it can be put in the middle of the oven.

Variation: Put 1 slice of ham in the buttered dish and heat for 1 minute at 490 (500) watts. Then put the egg on top and cook as described above. If using bacon, cook first for 2 (2½) minutes at 600 (500) watts.

Ramekin Eggs

Particularly fast

120 calories
Preparation time: 5 minutes
Cooking time: ½ minute

Serves: for 1 egg

1 tsp. butter

Salt, pepper

½ tsp. freshly chopped chervil

1 egg

1 small sprig chervil

Grease a small soufflé dish or ramekin with butter. Sprinkle a little salt, pepper and the chopped chervil on the base of the dish. Crack open the egg into the dish. Put the sprig of chervil on top. Cook the egg for ½ minute at 490 (500) watts, then let it stand for ½ minute. When placing on serving dish, tip the egg twice, so that the chervil remains on top.

Tip: If preparing 2 or 3 eggs at the same time, increase the cooking time for each egg by ½ minute. If the eggs are unevenly cooked, continue cooking for a little longer. The eggs look particularly attractive if cut out with a fluted pastry cutter. This method is useful for decorating a dish of vegetables.

Variations: Add 1 tbs. cream to the egg in the dish. Replace the chervil with tarragon or chopped chives. In addition, the egg will be more tasty if some chopped bacon or ham is sprinkled on it. Also, you can add 1 tsp. grated cheese or a small slice of cream cheese to the egg.

Scrambled Eggs

Good value

310 calories per serving
Preparation time: 5 minutes
Cooking time: 2½ (3) minutes

Serves: 2 people

1 tbs. butter

4 eggs

3 tbs. cream

Salt, pepper

1 tsp. chopped chives

Grease a soup bowl or a deep dish with some of the butter. Lightly mix the eggs with the cream and the remainder of the butter, season with salt and pepper. Put in the dish and cook for 1 (1¼) minutes at 600 (500) watts. Then continue cooking the eggs for 1½ (1¾) minutes at 600 (500), stirring them twice. Sprinkle with chives.

Tip: It is very important that the eggs are properly stirred, otherwise they dry out.

Variation: Cook 1 tsp. butter, 1 tsp. chopped shallot, ½ cup mushroom slices and 1 tsp. chopped parsley together for 1 (1¼) minutes at 600 (500) watts. Add to the eggs ½ minute before the end of their cooking time and stir.

Variation: Cook 2–3 tbs. fresh or frozen peas and 2–3 tbs. canned corn with 1 tsp. butter in a covered dish for ½ minute at 490 (500) watts. Mix with the eggs ½ minute before the end of their cooking time.

Variation: Add 1–2 skinned, cored and diced tomatoes and 1 tsp. chopped chives to the scrambled eggs ½ minute before the end of the cooking time. Serve on toast.

Sauces and Soups

While the main dish, for example, a large roast, is in the oven, soups, sauces and accompaniments can be prepared in the microwave oven with a minimum of effort. The advantages are obvious: nothing burns, nothing boils over and all the ingredients can be cooked simultaneously in the same attractive serving dish. The microwave oven is particularly useful for preparing soups for only a few people. For larger numbers it is better to cook them as usual and, if there are any left-overs, freeze them and later use the "fast wave" to defrost and heat up.

The risotto shown in the picture is excellent served with meat dishes of all sorts.

Once you have made a sauce in the microwave oven, you will never want to cook it in any other way. Everything can be completed in one operation (a quick stir is enough). There are no lumps, no skin, and you will be inspired by the delicious results.

Carrot Soup with Herbs

Good value

260 calories per serving
Preparation time: 15 minutes
Cooking time: 14 (16) minutes
Serves: 4 people

1¾ cups carrots
1 small potato
1 small onion
1 tbs. butter
1 tsp. chervil, freshly chopped
1 bacon rind
Salt, pepper
2 cups vegetable bouillon
½ cup cream
2 tbs. watercress, finely chopped
½ tbs. chopped chives

Peel and wash the carrots and potato and cut in thin slices. Peel and chop the onion. Put the butter, the carrots, the potato, the onion, the chervil and the bacon rind in a deep dish. Season with salt and pepper, cover and cook for 10 (11½) minutes at 600 (500) watts. Add the vegetable bouillon and cook for an additional 4 (4½) minutes at 600 (500) watts. Purée or liquidize. Add the cream and mix briefly again. Check seasoning. Pour soup into warmed plates and decorate with the mixed watercress and chives.

Tip: This soup can also be frozen, in which case do not add the cream until it is defrosted and re-heated. Celery soup can be made by the same method. The potato thickens the soup and gives it a pleasant aroma.

Green Pea Soup with Curry

More expensive

360 calories per serving
Preparation time: 20 minutes
Cooking time: 14 (16) minutes
Serves: 4 people

5 cups fresh peas
1 onion
1 tbs. butter
1 small piece root ginger, freshly grated, or ½ tsp. ground Ginger
½ tsp. curry powder
Pinch cayenne pepper
Salt, pepper
1½ cups chicken bouillon
½ cup cream
1 sprig fresh mint

Shell the peas. Peel and chop the onion and cook, covered, in the butter for 2 (2½) minutes at 600 (500) watts. Add the ginger, curry powder, cayenne pepper, a little salt and pepper, the peas and the chicken bouillon . Cover and cook for 12 (13½) minutes at 600 (500) watts. Liquidize the soup, then check seasoning. Whip the cream until stiff and mix half of it into the soup. Decorate the soup with the other half and garnish with the mint leaves.

Tip: This soup can also be prepared using frozen peas. In this case, shorten the cooking time by 2 (1¾) minutes. You can leave out the ginger and curry powder and substitute 1 tsp. finely chopped mint. In addition, the soup can be served with croûtons.

Fennel Soup with Lemon Balm

Good value

120 calories per serving
Preparation time: 15 minutes
Cooking time: 13 (15) minutes

Serves: 4 people

1¼ cups fennel	
½ onion	
Salt	
1 cup chicken bouillon	
½ cup cream	
Pepper	
Pinch cayenne pepper	
1 tbs. lemon balm, freshly chopped	

Trim off the leaves and wash the fennel, then cut in half lengthwise. Cut a third of it across in thin strips. Peel and chop the onion. Cook the fennel strips in 3 tbs. water and a little salt for 2 (2½) minutes at 600 (500) watts until just cooked. Finely chop the remainder of the fennel. Cook with the fennel leaves, the onion and the chicken bouillon for 11 (12½) minutes at 600 (500) watts. Purée the soup in a food processor. Whip the cream until stiff and mix into the soup with the fennel strips. Season with salt, pepper and cayenne pepper. Serve garnished with the chopped lemon balm.

Semolina Soup with Leeks

Very easy

75 calories per serving
Preparation time: 10 minutes
Cooking time: 11 (13) minutes

Serves: 4 people

¾ cup leeks	
1 tbs. butter	
Salt, pepper	
2 tbs. semolina made from durum wheat	
2 cup meat stock	

Wash the leeks, and cut in thin slices. Peel and chop the onion. Put the butter, the onion and the leeks in a deep dish. Season with a little salt and pepper and cook, covered, for 2 (2½) minutes at 600 (500) watts. Add the semolina and the meat stock and cook, uncovered, for 9 (10½) minutes at 600 (500) watts. Adjust seasoning and serve immediately.

Tomato Soup with Basil

Very easy

70 calories per serving
Preparation time: 15 minutes
Cooking time: 14 (16) minutes

Serves: 4 people

4 tomatoes	
1 onion	
2 cloves garlic	
1 tbs. butter	
1 tbs. freshly chopped basil	
1 tsp. tomato purée	
Pinch sugar	
2 cups beef bouillon	

Pour boiling water on the tomatoes, rinse in cold water, skin, core and chop finely. Peel the onion and the garlic. Chop the onion, press the garlic. Cook the butter, onion, garlic and tomatoes, covered, for 4 (4½) minutes at 600 (500) watts. Add the basil, tomato purée, sugar and beef bouillon and cook, uncovered, for 10 (11½) minutes at 600 (500) watts.

Cauliflower Soup with Broccoli

More difficult

110 calories per serving
Preparation time: 15 minutes
Cooking time: 18 (20½) minutes
Serves: 4 people

2¾ cups cauliflower	
1 tbs. butter	
1 tbs. parsley, freshly chopped	
½ cup milk	
2 cups hot chicken bouillon	
Salt, pepper	
Grated nutmeg	
1¾ cups broccoli	
3 tbs. water	

Divide the cauliflower into florets. Remove the stalk and leaves, wash the florets and put in a deep dish with the butter, parsley sand milk. Cover and cook until soft for 15 (17) minutes at 600 (500) watts. • Add the chicken bouillon, then purée in a mixer. Season the soup with salt, pepper and nutmeg. Wash the broccoli and divide into small florets. Cut the stalks into ½ in. slices. Put the broccoli and water, with a pinch of salt, in a dish and cook, covered, for 3 (3½) minutes at 600 (500) watts. Strain the broccoli. Put the broccoli stalks in the soup bowls or a tureen, pour over the soup and garnish with the broccoli florets.

Tip: This soup tastes particularly delicious if 2–3 tbs. stiffly whipped cream is added just before serving.

Minestrone

An Italian specialty

230 calories per serving
Soaking time: overnight
Preparation time: 25 minutes
Cooking time: 37 (41) minutes
Serves: 4 people

2 tbs. dried borlotti beans	
5 cups beef bouillon	
1 zucchini	
1 carrot	
1 root celeriac	
½ Savoy cabbage	
2 tomatoes	
1 onion	
1 clove garlic	
1 tbs. butter or olive oil	
1 tbs. basil, freshly chopped	
1 tsp. tomato purée	
1 small potato	
⅓ cup macaroni or small pasta shapes	
Salt, pepper	
Pinch sugar	

Soak the beans overnight in cold water. Then drain and cook, covered, in 2 cups beef bouillon for 10 minutes at 490 (500) watts. Wash and finely slice the zucchini, carrot and celeriac. Wash the cabbage leaves and cut in strips. Pour boiling water on to the tomatoes, skin and core them. Peel and chop the onion and garlic. Put all these ingredients into a large, deep dish with the butter or olive oil and cook, covered, for 2 (2½) minutes at 600 (500) watts. Add the basil, tomato purée and the remaining beef bouillon and cook for an additional 10 (11½) minutes at 600 (500) watts. Peel the potato and dice into small pieces. Add to the soup with the pasta and cook for 15 (17) minutes at 600 (500) watts. Season with salt, pepper and sugar.

French Onion Soup

A French specialty

260 calories per serving
Preparation time: 15 minutes
Cooking time: 25 (28) minutes

Serves: 3 people

2 cups onions
1 tbs. butter
3 slices French bread
2 tbs. clarified butter
6 tbs. white wine
½ tbs. beef bouillon
Pepper, grated nutmeg
½ cup Gruyère cheese, freshly grated

Peel and finely slice the onions and put in a deep dish with the butter. Cook for 6 (6½) minutes at 600 (500) watts, covered. Heat a browning dish for 5 (5½) minutes at 600 (500) watts. Put the bread slices with the clarified butter in this and

brown for 1½ (1¾) minutes at 600 (500) watts on each side. Add the white wine and the meat stock and cook, uncovered, for 10 (11½) minutes at 600 (500) watts. Season the soup with pepper and nutmeg and divide into bowls. Put the bread on top and sprinkle with the cheese. Melt the cheese for 1 minute at 490 (500) watts.

Zucchini Soup with Garlic

Very quick

70 calories per serving
Preparation time: 15 minutes
Cooking time: 11 (13) minutes

Serves: 3 people

2 cups zucchini
1 onion
1 clove garlic
1 tbs. butter
1½ cups beef bouillon
Salt, pepper

Wash and slice the zucchini. Peel and chop the onion. Peel and press the garlic. Cook the zucchini with the onion, garlic and butter, covered, for 9 (10½) minutes at 600 (500) watts. Add the beef bouillon and cook uncovered for 2 (2½) minutes at 600 (500) watts. Liquidize the soup in a processor, season to taste.

Vegetable Soup with Cheese

Good value

180 calories per serving
Preparation time: 20 minutes
Cooking time: 16 (18) minutes

Serves: 3 people

½ cup potatoes
½ cup leeks
½ cup celery
½ cup carrots
1 onion
2 lbs. butter
2 cups beef bouillon
1 bay leaf
1 clove
Salt, pepper
½ cup hard cheese, freshly grated

Clean the potatoes, leeks, celery and carrots and slice finely. Peel and chop the onion. Put all the ingredients in a deep dish with the butter and cook, covered, for 5 (5½) minutes 600 (500) watts. Add the beef bouillon, bay leaf and clove and cook for 10 (11½) minutes at 600 (500) watts. Season with salt and pepper. Sprinkle on the cheese and melt it for 1 minute at 490 (500) watts.

Swiss Barley Soup

Very easy; good value

450 calories per serving
Preparation time: 20 minutes
Cooking time: 68 (69½) minutes

Serves: 4 people

1 small carrot	
¼ cup celery	
1 small potato	
1 small leek	
2–3 Savoy cabbage leaves	
1 tbs. butter	
½ calves foot, cut in slices	
½ cup pearl barley	
4 cups beef bouillon	
1 onion	
1 bay leaf	
1 clove	
2 oz. smoked bacon	
Salt, pepper	
7 oz. smoked beef or pork	
1 egg yolk	
6 tbs. cream	

Peel the carrot, celery and the potato, wash and cut in small cubes. Trim the leek and the cabbage leaves, wash and cut in fine slices. Steam the butter with the vegetables and the calves foot slices for 4 (4½) minutes at 600 (500) watts. Add the barley and cook for 2 (2½) minutes at 600 (500) watts. Add half the bouillon. Peel the onion and use the clove to spike the bay leaf onto it. Cut the bacon into small squares. Add a little salt and pepper, the onion, the bacon and the smoked meat to the vegetables and cook for 60 minutes at 490 (500) watts. Add the remaining bouillon after the first 30 minutes. Remove the meat from the soup, cut it in small cubes and replace in soup. Mix the egg yolk with the cream and stir into the soup. Heat for 2 (2½) minutes at 600 (500) watts.

Piquant Cream of Celery Soup

More difficult; good value

160 calories per serving
Preparation time: 15 minutes
Cooking time: 19 (20½) minutes

Serves: 4 people

1 cup celery	
1 shallot	
1 tbs. butter	
1 tbs. flour	
4 cups beef or vegetable bouillon	
Salt, pepper	
Pinch cayenne pepper	
½ cup celery	
6 tbs. cream	
½ tbs. parsley, freshly chopped	

Peel 1 cup celery, wash and cut in small pieces. Peel the shallot and chop. Warm a large browning dish for 2 (2½) min-utes at 600 (500) watts. Let the butter melt in this. Add the shallot and 1 cup celery and dust with the flour. Cover and cook for 3 (3½) minutes at 600 (500) watts. Pour in the meat or vegetable stock and cook for 6 minutes, covered, at 490 (500) watts. Liquidize the soup and return to the dish. Season with salt, pepper and cayenne pepper. Trim ½ cup celery, wash and cut in very thin slices. Add to the soup and cook for 5 minutes at 490 (500) watts. Add the cream, check the seasoning and cook for an additional 3 (3½) minutes at 600 (500) watts. Sprinkle with parsley.

Tip: The shallot and celery can also be stewed in a normal dish with the butter. A browning dish, however, improves the flavor and color of the ingredients.

Liver Dumpling Soup

Good value

140 calories
Preparation time: 30 minutes
Cooking time: 12 (13¼) minutes

Serves: 4 people

6 oz. ox liver
¼ cup white bread
2 tbs. milk
1 small onion
1 tbs. parsley, freshly chopped
1 tsp. butter
1 egg
Breadcrumbs
Salt, pepper
1 tsp. dried marjoram
4 cups beef bouillon
1 tbs. chopped chives

Liquidize the liver in a food processor, then rub through a fine sieve. Break the bread in pieces and soak in the milk.

Squeeze out well and liquidize. Peel and finely chop the onion and put in a dish with the parsley and the butter. Cook for 1 (1¼) minutes at 600 (500) watts. Leave the mixture to cool, then mix with the egg, the liver and the bread. Add some breadcrumbs if necessary to make the mixture easy to shape. Season with salt, pepper and marjoram. Pour the stock in a large dish, cover and cook for 6 (6½) minutes at 600 (500) watts. Using two teaspoons, mold the liver mixture into small balls. Add these dumplings to the hot stock and cook for 5 (5½) minutes at 600 (500) watts. Pour the stock into warmed plates or soup cups and divide the dumplings between them. Serve sprinkled with the chives.

Tip: The dumplings will be easier to shape if you dip the spoons in hot water after making each one.

Goulash Soup

Very easy

260 calories per serving
Preparation time: 20 minutes
Cooking time: 19 (21) minutes

Serves: 2 people

¼ lb. beef
1 large onion
1 tbs. butter
1½ tbs. mild paprika powder
½ tbs. flour
1 tsp. tomato purée
4 cups beef bouillon
1 clove garlic
½ tsp. caraway seeds
Pinch dried marjoram
½ cup potatoes
½ green pepper
½ red pepper
Salt, pepper
2 pinches chili powder

Cut the meat in small cubes. Peel and chop the onion and put in a large dish with the meat and the butter. Stew for 3 (3½) minutes at 600 (500) watts. Dust the meat with the paprika and flour, and mix with the tomato purée. Cover and cook for 1 minute at 490 (500) watts. Combine the meat mixture with the bouillon. Peel and press the garlic and add to the mixture with the caraway seeds and marjoram. Cook covered for 6 minutes at 490 (500) watts. Meanwhile, peel and wash the potatoes, trim and wash the peppers, remove the seeds. Cut all three in small cubes and add to the soup. Cover and cook for 9 (10½) minutes at 600 (500) watts. Season with salt, pepper and chili powder.

Tip: Chili powder an be replaced by cayenne pepper.

Delicate Cream Sauce

Particularly quick

260 calories per serving
Preparation time: 5 minutes
Cooking time: 5½ (6¼) minutes

Serves: 2 people

1 shallot
2 tbs. white wine
3 tbs. beef or vegetable bouillon, or gravy
1¼ cups cream
Salt, pepper

Peel and finely chop the onion. Put the white wine in a dish with the gravy or stock and the onion and cook for 1½ (1¾) minutes at 600 (500) watts. Press the liquid through a sieve and replace in the dish. Mix in the cream and cook for 4 (4½) minutes at 600 (500) watts. Season with salt and pepper.

Tip: A light sauce can be improved with the addition of 1 tbs. vermouth and a brown sauce with 1 tbs. brandy.

Piquant White Wine Sauce

Very easy

310 calories per serving
Cooking time: 8 (9¼) minutes

Serves: 2 people

5 tbs. white wine
3 tbs. any bouillon or gravy
1¼ cups cream
1-2 tbs. butter
½ tsp. lemon juice (to taste)
Salt, pepper

Reduce approximately 3 tbs. white wine with the bouillon or gravy for 2 (2½) minutes at 600 (500) watts. Add the

cream and cook for an additional 5 (5½) minutes at 600 (500) watts. Cut the butter in small pieces and stir into the sauce. Add the remainder of the white wine and the lemon juice. Season with salt and pepper and finish cooking for 1 (1¼) minutes at 600 (500) watts.

Bechamel Sauce

Good value

285 calories per serving
Cooking time: 6½ (8) minutes

Serves: 2 people

¼ cup butter
¼ cup flour
2 cups milk
Salt, white pepper, grated nutmeg

Put the butter in a dish and melt for ½ (2½) minutes at 600 (500) watts, then stir well and cook for an additional 1 (1¼) minutes at 600 (500) watts. Stir the sauce well again, and cook for 3 (3½) minutes at 600 (500) watts. Season with salt, pepper and grated nutmeg.

Variations: Cook mixed herbs, capers or finely chopped vegetables, covered, for 1 (1¼) minutes at 600 (500) watts and mix into the sauce. Or, before the last cooking time, improve the sauce with 1–2 tbs. tomato purée and a pinch of sugar.

White Butter Sauce

Delicious

290 calories per serving
Preparation time: 5 minutes
Cooking time: 4½ (5¼) minutes

Serves: 3 people

1 shallot
1 tbs. white wine
1 tbs. fish or vegetable bouillon
3–4 crushed peppercorns
2 tbs. white wine vinegar
1 tbs. cream
½ cup butter
Salt, white pepper

Peel and chop the shallot. Reduce the white wine with the fish or vegetable bouillon, the peppercorns, the shallot and the vinegar for 3 (3½) minutes at 600 (500) watts until it measures about 3 tbs. Strain the mixture through a sieve and mix the liquid with the cream and ¼ cup of the butter, cut in small pieces. Heat for 1 minute at 490 (500) watts. Stir in the remaining butter and cook the sauce again for ½ (¾) minute at 600 (500) watts. Season to taste.

Hollandaise Sauce

Very quick

310 calories per serving
Cooking time: 3 (3¼) minutes

Serves: 3 people

½ cup butter
2 egg yolks
3 tbs. white wine
½ tsp. white wine vinegar
½ tsp. lemon juice
Salt, white pepper

Put the butter in a small dish and melt for 2 minutes at 490 (500) watts. Put the egg yolks, white wine, vinegar and lemon juice in a second dish and beat until frothy. Thicken the mixture for 1 (1¼) minutes at 360 (330) watts. Slowly add the melted butter to the egg mixture, stirring continuously. Season with salt and pepper.

Bearnaise Sauce

Slightly more expensive

310 calories per serving
Preparation time: 5 minutes
Cooking time: 5 minutes, 40 seconds (5 minutes, 50 seconds)

Serves: 3 people

1 shallot
½ cup butter
3 tbs. vinegar
1 tbs. water
1 tbs. tarragon, freshly chopped
1 tsp. chervil, freshly chopped
2 egg yolks
Salt, white pepper

Peel and chop the shallot. Put the butter in a small dish and melt for 2 minutes at 490 (500) watts. Cook the shallot with the vinegar, the water, half each of the tarragon and chervil, for 3 minutes at 490 (500) watts. Strain through a sieve and return to the dish. Beat the egg yolks and stir into the mixture. Thicken for 40 (50) seconds at 360 (330) watts. Stir the melted butter, drop by drop, into the mixture. Season with salt, pepper and the remaining herbs.

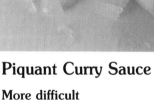

Piquant Curry Sauce

More difficult

95 calories per serving
Preparation time: 15 minutes
Cooking time: 12 (14) minutes

Serves: 4 people

1 onion
1 tbs. butter
2 tbs. curry powder
½ cup beef bouillon
½ cup milk
1 tsp. apricot jam
1 tsp. cornflour
3 tbs. pineapple juice
1 small apple
Salt, pepper
Pinch cayenne pepper

Peel and chop the onion, cook in the butter for 2 (2½) minutes at 600 (500) watts. Mix in the curry powder, the meat stock, the milk and the apricot jam. Mix the cornflour thoroughly with the pineapple juice. Peel and core the apple, then grate. Mix in the cornflour and grated apple. Cook for 7 (8) minutes at 600 (500) watts. Press the sauce through a fine sieve and cook for 3 (3½) minutes at 600 (500) watts. Season the sauce with salt, pepper, cayenne and, if necessary, some more curry powder.

Tip: This curry sauce goes well with poultry (chicken and turkey), veal, pork and fish (e.g. cod or angler fish). Suitable side dishes would be baked banana slices, roasted flaked almonds, raisins, finely diced bacon, chopped hardboiled egg, poached apple slices, pineapple pieces, desiccated coconut, and slightly crunchy rice.

Strong Red Wine Sauce

More expensive

85 calories per serving
Preparation time: 5 minutes
Cooking time: 18 (20½) minutes

Serves: 4 people

1 shallot
1 cup red wine
½ cup veal gravy or clear broth
2 tbs. butter
Salt, pepper

Peel and finely chop the shallot. Then add the red wine and cook for 10 (11½) minutes at 600 (500) watts until the liquid has reduced by half. Add the veal gravy or broth and reduce further for 5 (5½) minutes at 600 (500) watts. Stir in the butter in small pieces. Cook for 3 (3½) minutes at 600 (500) watts.

Season the sauce with salt and pepper.

Variations: For a brown cream sauce, replace the butter with some cream. A game sauce can be made in the same way. For a Madeira sauce, substitute 6 tbs. Madeira for the wine, and a little more broth or gravy. Stir in ½ tsp. tomato purée. For a Bordelaise sauce, substitute the pieces of butter with some finely chopped beef marrow and finally, mix in 1 tbs. chopped parsley.

Italian Tomato Sauce

Very easy; good value

110 calories per serving
Preparation time: 20 minutes
Cooking time: 12 (14) minutes

Serves: 4 people

1 onion
1 small carrot
1 piece celery
1 tbs. olive oil or butter
2–3 parsley stalks
5–6 basil leaves
1 bay leaf
1 small sprig thyme
5 cups peeled tomatoes (canned)
2 pinches meat extract or gravy granules
Salt, pepper, pinch sugar

P eel and finely chop the onion. Trim, wash and finely dice the carrot and celery. Put the butter or olive oil in a dish.

Add the onion, carrot, celery and herbs. Cook, covered, for 2 (2½) minutes at 600 (500) watts. Add the peeled tomatoes with their juice and the meat extract or gravy granules and cook for 10 (11½) minutes at 600 (500) watts. Press the mixture through a fine sieve. Season to taste with salt, pepper and sugar.

Tip: Ripe tomatoes can be used in summer.

Variation: Cook a finely chopped onion or a pressed clove of garlic with 1 tbs. olive oil, covered, for 2 (2½) minutes at 600 (500) watts, covered. Add 2 cups peeled, cored and diced tomatoes and cook for 5 minutes at 490 (500) watts. Purée in a processor and season with salt and pepper. This sauce goes particularly well with fish and other light dishes.

Bolognaise Sauce

More difficult; good value

220 calories per serving
Preparation time: 20 minutes
Cooking time: 17 (18½) minutes

Serves: 4 people

1 tbs. butter
1 onion
1 small carrot
1 small leek
1 piece celery
2 cloves garlic
7 oz. chopped beef
2 tbs. tomato purée
½ cup red wine
½ cup beef bouillon
1 bay leaf
1 tsp. marjoram, freshly chopped
1 tsp. parsley, freshly chopped
1 clove
Salt, pepper, pinch sugar

P ut the butter in a flat dish. Trim, wash and finely dice the onion, carrot, leek and celery. Peel and press the garlic and add to the butter with the vegetables. Cook, covered, for 2 (2½) minutes at 600 (500) watts. Add the beef to the vegetables and cook for 5 (5½) minutes at 600 (500) watts. Add the tomato purée, red wine, bouillon, herbs and clove, stir well and cook for 10 (10½) minutes at 360 (330) watts. Season the sauce with salt, pepper and sugar.

Saffron Risotto

An Italian specialty

380 calories per serving
Preparation time: 10 minutes
Cooking time: 18 (19¾) minutes

Serves: 3 people

1 onion
1 large tomato
1 tbs. olive oil or butter
1 cup short grain rice
1 cup beef bouillon
½ cup white wine
1 pinch saffron powder
2 tbs. butter
Salt, pepper
½ cup Parmesan cheese, freshly grated

Peel and chop the onion. Cube the skinned tomato. Mix the olive oil or butter, onion, tomato, rice, bouillon and ⅓ cup of the white wine in a dish. •

Cover and cook for 7 (8) minutes at 600 (500) watts. Then stir well and cook, covered, for 11 (11¾) minutes at 360 (330) watts. Stir the remaining white wine, the saffron and the butter, cut into small pieces, into the rice. Season with salt and pepper. Serve with the grated Parmesan.

Tip: There is no great saving of time to be achieved by cooking rice in the microwave oven. One advantage, however, is that all the ingredients can be put in one dish, after which there is no more preparation. Even the normal continuous stirring is unnecessary. This is also the ideal method for cooking novices. This simple risotto can also be made with mushrooms, tomatoes or green and red peppers, all of which are incorporated at the beginning.

Brown Rice Risotto

Good value

290 calories per serving
Soaking time: overnight
Preparation time: 5 minutes
Cooking time: 27 (36) minutes

Serves: 3 people

1 cup brown Italian rice
1 onion
1 tbs. butter or olive oil
⅓ cup vegetable or meat stock
6 tbs. white wine
1 tbs. butter
1 tbs. parsley, freshly chopped
Salt, pepper

Rinse the rice in cold water and soak overnight in ½ cup water. Peel and chop the onion. Put in a dish with the butter or olive oil, the stock, the drained rice and the white wine. • Cook, covered, for 7 (8) minutes at 600 (500) watts. Stir the

rice well and cook, covered, for an additional 20 (28) minutes at 490 (500) watts, stirring thoroughly twice more in the process. • Stir in the chopped butter and parsley and season the risotto with salt and pepper.

Tip: The best rice for preparing risotto and rice puddings is the Italian round grain rice called "Vialone." This is also available as brown rice. • The cooking time for rice in the microwave oven is somewhat shorter than for a conventional cooker. Another advantage is that cooking pots are unnecessary, as the whole risotto can be prepared in the serving dish. • Brown rice expands slightly less when cooked than polished rice, so it is advisable to measure out larger portions. As an accompaniment, allow ¼-½ cup per person and as a main dish ½-¾ cup per person.

Spaghetti Carbonara

An Italian speciality

900 calories per serving
Preparation time: 10 minutes
Cooking time: 21½ (23¾) minutes

Serves: 2 people

1 oz. smoked bacon
1 tbs. olive oil
½ cup cream
2 tbs. Parmesan cheese, freshly grated
4 cups water
1 tbs. salt
2 cups spaghetti
1 tbs. oil

Chop the bacon into small squares and heat with the olive oil for 1 minute at 490 (500) watts. • Add the cream and cheese and heat for ½ minute at 490 (500) watts. Cover the sauce and put to one side • Bring the water to a boil with the salt in a covered dish for 10 (11½) minutes at 600 (500) watts. Add the spaghetti and the oil and stir well. Cover and cook for 5 (5½) minutes at 600 (500) watts. Stir the spaghetti well and continue cooking for 4 (4½) minutes at 360 (330) watts. Then drain in a sieve. • Heat the sauce, covered, for 1 minute at 490 (500) watts and mix with the pasta.

Tip: The recipe for spaghetti carbonara is given instead of describing the cooking of plain spaghetti.

Variations: Cook the spaghetti as described above. Mix ½ cup cream with ¼ cup grated cheese and heat for ½ minute at 490 (500) watts. Mix with the drained spaghetti.

Polenta with Sage

Good value

310 calories per serving
Preparation time: 5 minutes
Cooking time: 7 (7¾) minutes

Serves: 3 people

2 cups vegetable or beef bouillon, or water
1 cup hominy grits, medium or coarse ground
3 tbs. butter
1 tsp. sage leaves
Salt, pepper

Mix the hominy grits with water or bouillon in a dish. Add 1 tbs. of the butter, cut in small pieces. Cover and cook for 2½ (3) minutes at 600 (500) watts. Then cook for an additional 3 minutes at 490 (500) watts, stirring, thoroughly, once during the cooking. Put the remaining butter with the sage leaves in a small dish. • Heat for 1½ (1¾) minutes at 600 (500) watts. Pour the butter through a sieve on to the polenta, season with salt and pepper, stir well and serve immediately.

Tip: Polenta is cooked relatively quickly in the microwave oven. Continuous stirring is avoided, as is the possibility that the grits will spit and jump. The polenta can also be put in a greased ring mold, left to stand for 1–2 minutes, then filled with stew. In addition, the polenta can be cooled, cut in slices and heated up in the microwave oven with butter for 1 (1¼) minutes at 600 (500) watts.

Cream Potatoes

Very easy

310 calories per serving
Preparation time: 10 minutes
Cooking time: 12 (13⅓) minutes

Serves 4 people

1 clove garlic	
2 cups potatoes	
Salt, white pepper	
Pinch grated nutmeg	
2¼ cups cream	
1 tbs. parsley	

Peel and halve the garlic and rub it round a shallow dish. Peel and wash the potatoes and cut in thin slices. Layer the slices in the dish. Sprinkle with salt, pepper and nutmeg. Pour the cream over the potatoes. • Cover the potatoes with cling film and cook for 12 (13½) minutes at 600 (500) watts. Sprinkle with chopped parsley.

Roasted New Poatoes

Very easy

180 calories per serving
Preparation time: 10 minutes
Cooking time: 13 (13½) minutes

Serves: 3 people

2¼ cups small new potatoes	
½ cup water	
Salt, pepper	
1 tbs. butter or clarified butter	

Wash the potatoes and scrape with a kitchen knife if necessary. Wash the potatoes again and dry. • Put in a suitable dish with the water and a little salt. Cover and cook for 4 minutes at 490 (500) watts. Drain the potatoes in a sieve. • Heat a browning dish for 4 (4½) minutes at 600 (500) watts, then melt the butter or clarified butter in this. Add the potatoes, season with salt and pepper and bake

for 5 minutes at 490 (500) watts. Turn the potatoes half-way through the cooking time.

Lyonnaise Potatoes

Good value

310 calories per serving
Preparation time: 10 minutes
Cooking time: 19 (20¼) minutes

Serves: 2 people

2 cups potatoes	
½ cup water	
1 large onion	
2 tbs. butter	
Salt, pepper	

Wash the potatoes and put them with the water in a suitable dish. Cover and cook for 8 minutes at 490 (500) watts. Put in a colander and leave to steam for a few moments. Heat a browning dish for 4 (4½) min-

utes at 600 (500) watts. Peel the potatoes and cut in ½ in. thick slices. • Peel and halve the onion and cut it in ¼ in. thick slices. Melt the butter in the browning dish. First add the onion then steam for 1 (1¼) minutes at 600 (500) watts. Add the potato slices, season with salt and pepper. Mix well and roast for 6 (6½) minutes at 600 (500) watts. Turn and stir well after half way through the cooking time.

Jacket Potatoes

Very easy

140 calories per serving
Preparation time: 5 minutes
Cooking time: 10 (11½) minutes

Serves 4 people:

3 cups medium sized potatoes
Salt

Thoroughly wash the potatoes, pierce well with a fork and place in a dish. Add a little salt and cook the potatoes, covered, for 10 (11½) minutes at 600 (500) watts. • Tip the potatoes into a colander and leave them to steam for a few moments.

Potato Purée

Good value

180 calories per serving
Preparation time: 15 minutes
Cooking time: 16 (17½) minutes

Serves: 4 people

3 cups potatoes
Salt, pepper
⅔ cup milk
1 tbs. cream
Grated nutmeg

Peel and wash the potatoes and cut them in 1 in. cubes. Put in a dish with 4 tbs. water, salt and pepper. Cover and cook for 10 minutes at 490 (500) watts. Drain in a colander and dry the cooking dish. Replace the potatoes in the dish and dry out for 2 (2½) minutes at 600 (500) watts. • Pass the potatoes through the finest blade of a mincer or a potato ricer. Heat the milk for 2 (2½) minutes at 600 (500) watts. Mix the potato purée with the milk and cream. Season with salt, pepper and nutmeg. • Reheat the purée before serving for 2 (2½) minutes at 600 (500) watts.

Potato Soup

Very easy

210 calories per serving
Preparation time: 20 minutes
Cooking time: 19 (19½) minutes

Serves: 4 people

1 small carrot
½ leek
1 small onion
1 small piece celery
3 cups potatoes
2 cups vegetable bouillon
1 tbs. butter
Salt, pepper
2 tsp. chopped chives

Peel and wash the carrot, cut in quarters lengthwise, and then into ¼ in. thick slices. Trim the leek, wash and cut in rings. Peel and chop the onion. Peel and finely chop the celery. Peel the potatoes and cut into 1 in. cubes. • Heat the vegetable bouillon for 6 (6½) minutes at 600 (500) watts. Add the butter, vegetables and potatoes. Cover and cook for 13 minutes at 490 (500) watts. Season with salt and pepper and sprinkle with the chives.

Fish and Seafood

Microwave ovens are ideal for the preparation of delicate fish. The tender flesh cannot tolerate lengthy cooking times and should not be allowed to dry out. Using a microwave oven, it is cooked to perfection in seconds or minutes and retains its typical flavor and attractive appearance. In no time at all you can conjure up appealing dishes with wonderful flavors, simply by adding chopped shallots, fresh herbs, a little butter or fine oil. If you wish to serve an exquisite sauce with your fish dish, it is no problem in the microwave. Even novices can prepare tasty sauces using the concentrated juices from the cooking process. The only prerequisite here, is that the recipes are followed exactly. Timing is essential in the cooking of both fish and sauces to ensure success. Whole fish can be cooked equally as successfully as fish filets in the microwave oven. A delicious gilt-head bream with mixed tomatoes, onions and herbs, as shown here in the picture, is a delicacy for fish lovers. It is important, however, that the fish should not be too big. If you have invited a larger number of people, first prepare one fish, wrap it in foil and set aside. Prepare the second fish.

Pike-Perch with Almonds

Slightly more expensive

360 calories per serving
Preparation time: 10 minutes
Cooking time: 9 minutes

Serves: 2 people

¾ lb. pike-perch filets (options: pike, grey mullet, perch, carp, turbot)

1 tsp. lemon juice
1 tsp. Worcestershire sauce
Salt, pepper
2 tbs. butter
2 tbs. flour
2 tbs. flaked almonds
1 tbs. chopped chives

Cut the fish filets in 4-6 pieces. Sprinkle with lemon juice and Worcestershire sauce, then with salt and pepper. Pre-heat a browning dish for 5 (5½) minutes at 600 (500) watts. Add half of the butter. Dry the pieces of fish with paper towel, coat with the flour and cook, covered, for 2 minutes at 490 (500) watts. Turn over after half way through the cooking time. Put the fish on warmed plates. Roast the almonds in the remainder of the butter for 2 (2½) minutes at 600 (500) watts until golden brown. Add the chives and pour the mixture over the fish filets.

Tip: The almonds can also be roasted without fat. Pre-heat the browning dish for 5 (5½) minutes at 600 (500) watts, add the flaked almonds and roast for 2 (2½) minutes until golden brown. Turn after half of the cooking time. Whole trout or any favorite fish filets can be prepared the same way. When cooking whole fish the cooking time should be increased according to the size of the fish.

Perch Filets with Capers and Nuts

Very quick

450 calories per serving
Preparation time: 10 minutes
Cooking time: 2½ minutes

Serves: 2 people

Salt, pepper
10 oz. skinned perch filets
1 tsp. lemon juice
½ tsp. soy sauce
¼ cup butter
1 tbs. walnut, freshly chopped
1 tbs. capers
1 tsp. chopped chives

Sprinkle salt and pepper on both sides of the filets, then lemon juice and soy sauce. Grease a shallow dish with 1 tbs. of the butter. Lay the filets side by side in the dish. Cut the remaining butter in pieces and spread over the fish with the walnuts and capers. Cook, covered, for 2½ minutes at 490 (500) watts. Serve on warm plates and sprinkle with chives.

Tip: Whitefish and pike-perch filets can also be prepared in the same way.

Trout Mousse

More demanding

130 calories per serving
Preparation time: 30 minutes
Chilling time: 1½ hours
Cooking time: 4 (4¾ minutes)

Serves: 6 people

| 1 tbs. butter |
| ½ lb. trout filets |
| Salt, pepper |
| 5 tbs. red wine |
| 3 tbs. fish bouillon or vegetable bouillon |
| 1 tsp. cornflour |
| 1 tomato |
| 4 basil leaves |
| 1 tbs. gelatin |
| ½ cup cream |

Butter a dish. Cut the trout filets in pieces, place in a dish and season with salt and pepper. Add about 3 tbs. of the red wine and cook, covered, for

1½ minutes at 490 (500) watts. Pour off the wine into a small dish, stir in the fish or vegetable stock and cornflour and cook for 2 (2½) minutes at 600 (500) watts. Cool this mixture and add to the fish. Pour boiling water over the tomato, skin and core it. Wash the basil leaves and tear them into small pieces. Leave all these ingredients to cool for 30 minutes, then purée in processor. • Cook the remaining red wine for ½ (¾) minutes at 600 (500) watts. Then dissolve the gelatin in the red wine. Stir this into the fish mixture. Whip the cream until stiff and fold it into the mixture. Season to taste with salt and pepper. Put the mixture into a dish, smooth the top and leave to set in the fridge for 1 hour.

Blue Trout

Very easy

600 calories per serving
Preparation time: 15 minutes
Cooking time: 20½ (22¾) minutes

Serves: 2 people

| 1 piece celery |
| ½ leek |
| 1 small onion |
| 2–3 parsley stalks |
| 4 cups water |
| ¼ cup white wine |
| 1 tbs. salt |
| 4–5 peppercorns |
| 2 prepared trout, each weighing 9–10 oz. |
| ¼ cup white wine vinegar |
| ⅓ cup butter |

Peel, wash and finely cube the celery. Trim, wash and finely chop the leek. Peel and coarsely chop the onion. Rinse

the parsley in cold water. Cook all these ingredients with the water, wine, salt and peppercorns in a large dish for 11 (12½) minutes at 600 (500) watts. • Baste the trout with the vinegar. Add to the white wine mixture and cook, covered, for 8 (8½) minutes at 360 (330) watts. Remove the trout from the oven and keep warm in the bouillion. Put the butter in a dish and heat for 1½ (1¾) minutes at 600 (500) watts. Drain the trout and serve with the melted butter.

Tip: It is important to be careful not to wash off the slimy layer on the skin while preparing the fish in this way, otherwise the fish will not become blue. • The fish are cooked when the dorsal fin can be easily pulled away from the body.

Angler Fish with Spinach

More expensive

330 calories per serving
Preparation time: 15 minutes
Cooking time: 4 (4½) minutes

Serves: 2 people

⅓ cup butter
⅓ cup leaf spinach, weighed after trimming
1 clove garlic
Salt, pepper
½ lb. angler fish filets (options: sea bass, sea bream, small octopus)
2 tbs. white wine

Grease a dish with some of the butter. Wash the spinach and cut in fine strips. Put these in the dish. Peel and press the garlic and sprinkle over the spinach. Season with a little salt and pepper. Cut the fish filets into ½ in. thick slices, sprinkle with salt and pepper, and arrange on top of the spinach. • Pour the white wine over and cook, covered, for 2½ minutes at 490 (500) watts. Take the fish and spinach out of the dish and arrange on plates. Reduce the cooking liquid by cooking with 2 tbs. of the butter for 1 (1¼) minutes at 600 (500) watts. • Cut the remaining butter in small pieces and stir in with an egg whisk. Season the sauce with salt and pepper and pour over the fish. Heat the fish, covered, for ½ (¾) minutes at 600 (500) watts before serving.

Tip: For a colorful effect, peel and core a tomato, cut it in small cubes and garnish the fish with it. Some chopped tarragon can be added to the butter sauce.

Sole and Salmon in Cabbage Parcels

More expensive

310 calories per person
Preparation time: 20 minutes
Cooking time: 14½ (16¼) minutes

Serves: 4 serving

4 large Savoy cabbage leaves
1 cup water
Salt
4 slices salmon
4 sole filets
2 tbs. butter
Pepper
Juice of 1 lemon
1 shallot
½ cup cream
2 tbs. white wine
1 tbs. parsley, finely chopped
1 tbs. chervil, finely chopped

Wash the cabbage leaves and cook, covered, in the water with a pinch of salt for 7 (8) minutes at 600 (500) watts. Put the salmon slices and sole filets in a shallow buttered dish, season with salt and pepper and sprinkle over with the lemon juice. • Drain the cabbage leaves well and spread out on the work surface. If necessary, cut the thick veins at intervals. Roll up each sole filet and wrap them around with the salmon slices. Then wrap them in the cabbage leaves. • Peel and finely chop the shallot and cook with the cream for 4 (4½) minutes at 600 (500) watts. Add the wine, cabbage rolls and herbs, and cook, covered, for 1½ minutes at 490 (500) watts. Take out the cabbage rolls and keep warm. Cut the remaining butter in small pieces and add to the sauce. Cook for an additional 1 (1¼) minutes at 600 (500) watts. Sea-

son the sauce with salt and pepper and arrange on plates with the cabbage rolls.

Ocean Perch Filets with Cress Sauce

Very easy

450 calories per serving
Preparation time: 10 minutes
Cooking time: 6½ (7½) minutes

Serves: 2 people

1 tsp. butter
2 tbs. white wine
4–6 ocean perch filets (options: redfish, rose fish) (11 oz.)
3 tbs. cress
3 tbs. butter
6 tbs. cream
Salt, pepper

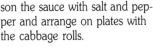utter a dish with 1 tsp. butter. Pour in the white wine and cook for ½ (¾) minute at 600 (500) watts, until reduced

by half. Add the fish filets and cook, covered, for 3 (3¼) minutes at 360 (330) watts. Cut the cress from the bed, wash, chop and knead with the butter. • Take out the fish filets and keep warm. Reduce the cream for 3 (3½) minutes at 600 (500) watts. Stir in the cress butter. Season the sauce with salt and pepper, pour on to the warmed plates and arrange the fish filets on top.

Tip: Ocean perch filets should only be scaled, not skinned. The beautiful red skin is typical of this fish and strengthens its individual flavor. Ocean perch filets also look more attractive if they are served with the skin on top. • The cress can be replaced by other herbs, for instance, in Spring wild garlic, sorrel or young stinging nettles. These herbs, however, have a stronger flavor, so should be used in smaller quantities.

Turbot or Flounder/Sole with Red Wine Sauce

Very easy

430 calories per serving
Preparation time: 10 minutes
Cooking time: 11 (12¼) minutes

Serves: 2 people

2 turbot filets (about 9–9¼ oz.)
Salt, pepper
1–2 tsp. lemon juice
1 shallot
½ cup red wine
⅓ cup butter

Season the filets on both sides with salt and pepper and sprinkle with 1 tsp. lemon juice. • Peel and finely chop the shallot and cook with 5 tbs. of the red wine for 6 (6½) minutes at 600 (500) watts until the liquid is slightly reduced. • Cut the fish filets in half across, place in the red wine sauce and cook,

covered, for 2 (2¼) minutes at 360 (330) watts. Take out the filets and arrange on warmed plates. Strain the liquid through a sieve and replace in the dish with the remaining wine. Reduce this stock by cooking for 3 (3½) minutes at 600 (500) watts. Stir the butter, cut in small pieces, into the sauce. Season with salt and pepper, and according to taste, a little lemon juice. Pour sauce over 1 filet on each plate and arrange the other diagonally across it.

Tip: For best results, buy one filet with black skin and one with white, so that the dish can be presented attractively. The white skin is removed before cooking, the black skin left. When arranging the food, the skinned filet is placed on the plate first, some sauce is poured over it, and it is then covered by the second filet. The skin can be easily pulled off before eating.

Cod in Cider

More difficult

330 calories per serving
Preparation time: 15 minutes
Cooking time: 11 (12½) minutes

Serves: 2 people

1 medium-sized onion
1 clove garlic
1 tbs. olive oil
2 cod cutlets, each about 6 oz.
2 tbs. freshly chopped parsley
Salt, pepper
1 cup cider
1 tsp. cornstarch
1 tbs. cream
1 hard-boiled egg
6 cooked asparagus tips

Peel and finely chop the onion and garlic. Heat a browning dish for 2 (2½) minutes at 600 (500) watts. Add the olive oil and onion. Steam for 1 minute at 490 (500) watts. Add the fish, parsley and garlic. Steam for 1 (1¼) minutes at 600 (500) watts. Remove the fish, season with salt and pepper and keep warm. Pour about ¾ cup of the cider on to the onion and cook for 3 (3½) minutes at 600 (500) watts until reduced by half. • Mix the remaining cider well with the cornstarch. Add to the sauce and thicken for 1 minute at 490 (500) watts. Season with salt and pepper. Put the fish in the sauce and heat for 3 (3¼) minutes at 360 (330) watts. Add the cream and arrange everything on warmed plates. Garnish with quartered hard-boiled eggs and asparagus tips.

Cod with Tomatoes and Peas

More expensive

360 calories per serving
Preparation time: 30 minutes
Cooking time: 27 (30½) minutes

Serves: 4 people

1 onion
2 cloves garlic
1 carrot
4 large cod cutlets
Salt, pepper
1 cup white wine
10 oz. or 2¼ cups fish bones
1 tbs. flour
2 tbs. olive oil
2¼ cups tomatoes
1¾ cups fresh, podded peas
1 tbs. mixed herbs, freshly chopped
1 tsp. paprika
1 little saffron

Peel and chop the onion and garlic. Trim the carrot and cut in thin slices. Season the fish with salt and pepper, sprinkle with 2–3 tbs. of the wine and leave in a cool place for 10 minutes. • Wash the fish bones and cook for 7 (8) minutes at 600 (500) watts with the water, onion, garlic and carrot. Then strain and reduce the liquid for 8 (9) minutes at 600 (500) watts. Pat the fish dry and coat with the flour. Place it in the browning dish with the olive oil and cook for 2 (2½) minutes at 600 (500) watts on each side. Pour boiling water on to the tomatoes, skin and finely dice them and add to the fish with the peas, herbs and paprika. Steam for 2 minutes at 490 (500) watts. Pour over 6 tbs. fish stock and the remaining wine and cook for 6 (6½) minutes at 360 (330) watts. Season the dish with salt, pepper and saffron.

Lukewarm Fish Salad

More expensive

210 calories per serving
Preparation time: 30 minutes
Cooking time: 7½ (8¼) minutes

Serves: 4 people

¼ lb. boned angler fish (monk fish)
¼ lb. boned salmon
3 oz. prawns
4 scallops
1 shallot
3 tbs. olive oil
Salt, pepper
½ tsp. freshly chopped tarragon
1 tbs. sherry vinegar
Pinch cayenne pepper
4 tarragon sprigs
4 lemon wedges
A few saffron threads

Cut the angler (monk) fish and salmon into four slices each. If not devined, shell the prawns apart from the tail. Remove the intestine. Trim the scallops, remove the corals (roe-American, use for a soup), and cut flesh in half across. Peel and chop the shallot. • Heat a browning dish for 3 (3½) minutes at 600 (500) watts. Grease with a little of the olive oil. Put the fish pieces, the prawns and scallops in the dish and steam for 1½ (1¾) minutes at 600 (500) watts. Take out the fish and season with salt and pepper. Put the shallot and tarragon in the cooking liquid and cook, covered, for 2 minutes at 490 (500) watts. Add the remaining olive oil and sherry vinegar. Heat for 1 minute at 490 (500) watts. Mix everything well and season with a little salt and cayenne pepper. Arrange the fish on 4 warmed plates and pour over the sauce. Decorate each with 1 sprig tarragon, 1 lemon wedge and some saffron threads.

Fish with Lime Sauce

More difficult

310 calories per serving
Preparation time: 30 minutes
Cooking time: 16 (18) minutes

Serves: 4 people

2 cups water
1 shallot
2 limes
1 lobster tail
2 tbs. butter
2 sole filets (3 oz. each)
4 slices sea perch (1½ oz. each)
2 slices salmon (1½ oz. each)
1 tsp. cornstarch
1 tbs. white wine
2 tbs. lime juice
6 tbs. cream
Salt, pepper

Boil the water for 6 (6½) minutes at 600 (500) watts. Peel and finely chop the shallot. Skin the limes, divide into segments and remove the skin from the segments. Cube half of these. • Cook the lobster tail, covered, in boiling water for 3 (3½) minutes at 600 (500) watts. Cool and shell. Heat a browning dish for 2 (2½) minutes at 600 (500) watts. Add half the butter and the fish pieces and steam for 1 minute at 490 (500) watts. Cover the fish and keep warm. Steam the lime cubes and shallot in the cooking liquid for 2 minutes at 490 (500) watts. • Stir the cornstarch into the white wine and lime juice and put in the dish with the cream. Cook the sauce for 2 (2½) minutes at 600 (500) watts. Beat the remaining butter into the sauce, a piece at a time. Season the sauce with salt and pepper, pour on to warmed plates and arrange the fish on top. Garnish with the lime segments.

Fish Terrine with Caviar

More difficult

240 calories per serving
Preparation time: 30 minutes
Chilling time: 30 minutes
Cooking time: 6 (7) minutes

Serves: 6 people

3 cups water
Salt
¼ cup leaf spinach, weighed after trimming
½ tbs. butter
9 oz. filets (options: *sole, flounder*)
6 oz. salmon filets
Pepper
Juice of 1 lemon
1 egg white
1¼ cups cream
1 tbs. dry vermouth
2 tbs. red caviar
1 egg yolk
2 dill sprigs

Boil the salted water in a pot on the stove. Wash the spinach, put in the hot water for 10 seconds. Pour into a sieve and rinse with cold water. Drain well and spread out on a plate. Dry well with kitchen paper. Grease a small terrine (about 7 in. long) with the butter. Line the terrine with some of the spinach. • Keep one flounder or sole filet whole and cut the rest into chunks. Cut a piece of salmon the length of the terrine and ¾ in. wide. Cut the remainder into small pieces. Put the two types of fish in separate dishes, sprinkle with salt, pepper and the lemon juice and put in the fridge for 30 minutes. Likewise, cool all the other ingredients. • Liquidize the flounder/sole with the egg white, 3 tbs. of the cream and the vermouth. Stir the red caviar into the mixture. Season with salt and pepper. Liquidize the salmon with the remainder of the cream and the

egg yolk and season with salt and pepper. • First put a ⅛ in. thick layer of the white mixture in the terrine, followed by a layer of pink mousse and a dill sprig. Wrap the strip of salmon in the whole filet and place in the middle of the terrine. Cover with the remaining salmon mousse and the second dill sprig. Spread the rest of the white mixture over the top, and cover with the remaining spinach leaves. Cover and cook the terrine for 4 (3½) minutes at 600 (500) watts. Let the terrine rest for 4 minutes, then cook again for 3 (3½) minutes at 600 (500) watts. • The terrine can be served hot or cold. To serve, turn out and cut in ½-¾ in. thick slices. • The mixtures can also be put lengthwise in the terrine, which is simpler but not so attractive.

Tip: Immediately after cooling the terrine, put it in the refridgerator. It will keep for 2 days. A cocktail sauce goes particularly well with this.

Fish Timbales with a Surprise Filling

More expensive

150 calories per serving
Preparation time: 30 minutes.
Cooking time: 4½ (5) minutes

Serves: 4 people

7 oz. fish fillets, e.g. grey mullet
Salt, pepper
1 tsp. lemon juice
4 tbs. cream
A few saffron threads
1 egg white
1 tbs. Pernod
1 tbs. butter
4 tsp. caviar or lumpfish roe

Cut the filets in strips. Sprinkle with salt, pepper and lemon juice and leave in a cool place for about 10 minutes. Boil the cream with the saffron for 2 (1½) minutes at 600 (500) watts, then leave to cool. • Purée in the food processor, the saffron cream, filets, egg white and Pernod. Grease 4 small soufflé dishes (about 2¾ in.) with the butter. Fill each ¾ with the mixture. Make a hollow in each one with a teaspoon, place 1 tsp. of caviar in each hollow, then top with a little fish mixture. Bang each dish on a folded cloth several times, so that the mixture is well distributed and any air bubbles are knocked out. Cover the dishes with plastic wrap and cook the fish mixture for 2½ minutes at 490 (500) watts. Leave to rest for 3–5 minutes, then turn out on to warmed plates and garnish.

Tip: The ingredients for this dish should be well chilled before mixing, otherwise the mixture will not be smooth. A dry wine or champagne sauce goes well with this dish.

Flounder/Sole with Green Peppercorns

Very fast

520 calories per serving
Preparation time: 10 minutes
Cooking time: 9 (10) minutes

Serves: 2 people

2 prepared flounder or sole, each weighing about 10 oz.
1 tbs. butter
2 shallots
1 clove garlic
½ cup mushrooms
2 tsp. green peppercorns in brine
2 tbs. mixed herbs (e.g. parsley, chervil, chives), finely chopped
2 tbs. white wine
1 tsp. soy sauce
1 tsp. lemon juice
Salt, pepper

U sing a pointed knife, cut several slits on both sides of each fish. Grease 2 shallow dishes with 2 tsp. butter each. Peel and chop the shallots and garlic. Trim the mushrooms and cut in thin slices. • Mix the shallots, garlic and mushrooms with the peppercorns, which have been rinsed in cold water, and divide between the dishes. Place 1 fish in each, sprinkle with white wine, soy sauce and lemon juice, then season with salt and pepper. Cook 1 fish for 4 (4½) minutes at 360 (330) watts, covered, then the other. Before serving, heat the first fish for 1 minute at 490 (500) watts.

Mackerel with Tomatoes

Very easy

690 calories per serving
Preparation time: 35 minutes
Cooking time: 10 (11) minutes

Serves: 2 people

1 prepared mackerel (about 1 lb.)
Salt, pepper
1 tsp. lemon juice
3 cloves garlic
3 tbs. olive oil
5 tomatoes
1 shallot
2 tbs. freshly chopped parsley
1 small zucchini
1 tbs. tomato purée

C ut slits at ¼-½ in. intervals on both sides of the fish near the backbone with the point of a knife. Rub salt, pepper and lemon juice into the fish. Peel 2 garlic cloves and cut in slices. Put one slice into each of the slits in the fish. Place the fish in a dish and sprinkle with 1 tsp. of the olive oil. Leave to rest for 15 minutes. • Meanwhile, pour boiling water over the tomatoes, peel and core, then cut in small cubes. Peel the shallot and remaining clove of garlic and chop finely. Mix with the parsley. Trim, wash and thinly slice the zucchini. • Put the parsley mixture and the remaining olive oil in a dish and cook, covered, for 2 (2½) minutes at 600 (500) watts. Add the tomatoes and tomato purée. Put the mackerel on top and cook, covered, for 8 (8½) minutes at 360 (330) watts. Before cutting up the fish for serving, remove the garlic slices.

Cod with Potatoes and Peppers

Good value

500 calories per serving
Preparation time: 30 minutes
Cooking time: 20 (20½) minutes

Serves: 2 people

1 lb. 2 oz. cod (tail portion)
Salt, pepper
1 tsp. Worcestershire sauce
1 tsp. lemon juice
2 tbs. butter
1 onion
1 clove garlic
1 small red chili
2 large potatoes
1 cup green, red or yellow peppers
3 tbs. white wine
3 tbs. meat stock
2 tbs. parsley, freshly chopped

Season the cod with salt, pepper, Worcestershire sauce and lemon juice. Grease a large dish with half of the butter. Peel, halve and finely slice the onion. Peel and press the garlic. Add both to the dish. Wash and core the chili, chop it and sprinkle on top. Peel, wash and thinly slice the potatoes and arrange in overlapping slices around the edge of the dish. Wash, halve, core the peppers and cut them in ⅛ in. wide strips. Put in the middle of the dish. Season these vegetables with salt and pepper, then pour over the white wine and stock. Cover and cook the vegetables for 11 minutes at 490 (500) watts. • Place the fish on top and cook for 9 (9½) minutes at 360 (330) watts. • One minute before the end of the cooking time, add the remaining butter, cut in small pads, to the fish. Serve sprinkled with the parsley.

Herring Rolls with Apple

Very quick

860 calories per serving
Preparation time: 15 minutes
Cooking time: 1 (1¼) minute(s)

Serves: 2 people

6 fresh herring filets (about 1¼ lbs.)
Salt, pepper
1 tsp. Worcestershire sauce
2 tbs. apple or white wine vinegar
Juice of 1 lemon
1 apple
1 large onion
1 tbs. parsley, freshly chopped
Pinch cayenne pepper
1 tbs. sunflower or grapeseed oil
½ cup green salad (e.g. endive, lettuce or watercress)

Lay the herring filets in a shallow dish, add salt, pepper and sprinkle with the Worcestershire sauce and apple or white wine vinegar and the lemon juice. • Peel, core and grate the apple. Peel and halve the onion, then slice thinly. Take the herring filets out of the marinade. • Mix the apple with the parsley, onion slices and marinade. Season with salt and cayenne pepper. • Lay out the filets with the skin side down and divide the filling between them. Roll up each filet and secure with a wooden toothpick. • Place the rolls in a dish. Sprinkle with the sunflower or grapeseed oil and cook, covered, for 1 (1¼) minutes at 600 (500) watts. Garnish the rolls with the salad. Fresh crusty bread is the ideal accompaniment.

Tip: This recipe is equally successful using white herring filets.

Mariner-Style Mussels

Very easy

570 calories per serving
Preparation time: 20 minutes
Cooking time: 11 (12) minutes

Serves: 2 people

3¼ lbs. mussels
4 shallots
1 tbs. butter
2 cups white wine
1 bay leaf
2–3 parsley stalks
1 small sprig thyme
Salt, black pepper
Juice of ½ lemon
2 tbs. parsley, freshly chopped

With the cold tap running, clean the mussels thoroughly with a brush. Pull out the "beard." • Peel and chop the shallots and cook, covered, in a

large dish with the butter for 2 (2½) minutes at 600 (500) watts. Add the wine, mussels, bay leaf, herbs, a little salt, and a lot of pepper. Cook, covered for 7 minutes at 490 (500) watts. • Divide the mussels between 2 heated plates. • Reduce the remaining cooking liquid by cooking with the lemon juice for 2 (2½) minutes at 600 (500) watts. Pour over the mussels. Serve, sprinkled with parsley.

Mussels (Clams) in Curry Sauce

More difficult

645 calories per serving
Preparation time: 25 minutes
Cooking time: 10 (10½) minutes

Serves: 2 people

3¼ lbs. mussels
2 cloves garlic
1 onion
1 tbs. parsley, freshly chopped
1½ tbs. butter
½ cup white wine
½ cup cream
1 tsp. cornstarch
Salt, pepper
½ tsp. curry powder

With the cold tap running, clean the mussels thoroughly with a brush. Pull out the "beard." • Peel and press the garlic. Peel and chop the onion.

Steam both with the parsley and butter by cooking in a large covered dish for 2 (2½) minutes at 600 (500) watts. Add the mussels and white wine, cover and cook for 7 minutes at 490 (500) watts. • Drain the mussels and divide between warmed plates. Mix the cream with the cornstarch, a little salt, pepper and the curry powder and stir thoroughly into the cooking liquid. Cook the sauce for 1 minute at 490 (500) watts.

Mussels with Vegetable Sauce

More difficult

450 calories per serving
Preparation time: 35 minutes
Cooking time: 16½ (18) minutes

Serves: 3 people

3¼ lbs. mussels	
½ leek	
1 small carrot	
1 shallot	
1½ tbs. butter	
Salt, pepper	
½ cup white wine	
½ cup cream	
1 egg yolk	
1 tbs. dry vermouth	

With the cold tap running, brush the mussels until thoroughly clean. Pull out the "beard." Wash and trim the leek, peel the carrot and cut both in thin strips resembling matchsticks. Peel and chop the shallot, then put in a large dish with the other vegetables, butter, salt and pepper and white wine. Cover and steam for 3 (3½) minutes at 600 (500) watts. • Add the mussels and cook, covered, for an additional 7 minutes at 600 (500) watts. Divide the mussels between warmed plates. Reduce the cooking liquid for 4 (4½) minutes at 600 (500) watts. Pour in the cream and cook the sauce for 2 (2½) minutes at 600 (500) watts. • Stir the egg yolk into the vermouth. Mix into the sauce and thicken for ½ minute at 490 (500) watts. Pour the sauce over the mussels.

Stuffed (Clams) Mussels

Very easy

670 calories per serving
Preparation time: 35 minutes
Cooking time: 10 (10½) minutes

Serves: 2 people

2¼ lbs. mussels	
1 shallot	
1 clove garlic	
½ cup white wine	
Pepper	
For the stuffing:	
2 tomatoes	
2 cloves garlic	
2 tbs. breadcrumbs	
2 tbs. freshly chopped parsley	
3 tbs. white wine	
5 tbs. olive oil	
Salt, pepper	
Pinch cayenne pepper	

Brush the mussels thoroughly under cold running water. Pull out the "beard." Put the mussels in a deep dish. Peel the shallot and 1 garlic. Chop the shallot and press the garlic. Add both to the mussels with the white wine and pepper. • Cover and cook for 7 minutes at 490 (500) watts. Drain the mussels well. Remove 1 shell from each. Divide the shells still containing flesh between 2 large plates. Pour boiling water over the tomatoes, peel and core them and cut in small cubes. Peel the garlic and press. Mix both with the breadcrumbs, parsley, white wine and olive oil. Season well with salt, pepper and cayenne pepper. Put in the empty mussel shells. Heat each portion separately, uncovered, for 1½ (1¾) minutes at 360 (330) watts.

Oysters with Hollandaise Sauce

More expensive

550 calories per serving
Preparation time: 30 minutes
Cooking time: 5¼ (6¼) minutes

Serves: 2 people

12 deep oysters
½ cup butter
2 egg yolks
3 tbs. white wine
½ tsp. white wine vinegar
1 tsp. chervil, freshly chopped
1 tsp. lemon juice
Salt, pepper
Pinch cayenne pepper

Open the oysters, detach the flesh and remove the sinews. Rinse out the shells and dry well, so that no juice remains inside which might thin the sauce. Put the butter in a dish and heat for 1½ (1¾) minutes at 600 (500) watts. • Put the egg yolks, white wine, vinegar, chervil and lemon juice in a dish and thicken for ¾ (1) minute at 360 (330) watts. Slowly stir in the melted butter. Season with salt and pepper. • Put 6 oysters in the deeper halves of the shells. Pour 1 tbs. sauce over each and heat the oysters for 1½ (1¾) minutes at 360 (330) watts. • Repeat with the other 6 oysters. • Sprinkle the oysters with cayenne pepper and serve immediately.

Tip: Instead of cayenne pepper, caviar can be put on top of the oysters. The oyster juice is removed from this dish so that it is not too salty. Oysters can be opened easily by putting them in the microwave oven for 1 minute at "defrost."

Giant Shrimp or Prawns with Whisky Sauce

More expensive

430 calories per serving
Preparation time: 5 minutes
Cooking time: 11 (12¼) minutes

Serves: 2 people

10-12 giant prawns or shrimp
1 shallot
2 tbs. white wine
2 tbs. whisky
½ tsp. lemon juice
1 tsp. Worcestershire sauce
Salt, pepper
½ cup cream
1 tbs. chicken stock or bouillon
Pinch cayenne pepper
A little additional whisky

Put the prawns or shrimp in a large dish. Peel and chop the shallot and add to the prawns. Sprinkle with the white wine, whisky, lemon juice and Worcestershire sauce. Season with salt and pepper. • Cover and cook for 6 (6½) minutes at 360 (330) watts. Turn after half the cooking time, bringing the bottom ones to the top. • Pour off the cooking liquid. Cover the prawns and keep warm. Reduce the stock for 4 (4½) minutes at 600 (500) watts. Stir in the cream and chicken stock and cook for another 1 (1¼) minutes at 600 (500) watts. Season the sauce with cayenne pepper and finally a little whisky.

Tip: Thaw deep frozen prawns or shrimp for 7-8 minutes using the "defrost" cycle. Leave for 10 minutes after this. When using prawns without heads, reduce the thawing time by 2 minutes.

Scampi with Lemon Sauce

More difficult

480 calories per serving
Preparation time: 20 minutes
Cooking time: 6 (6¾) minutes

Serves: 2 people

10 large scampi (emperor prawns) with shells
1 tsp. soy sauce
4½ tbs. lemon juice
Salt, pepper
3 tbs. butter
½ cup cream
Pinch cayenne pepper
1 tsp. mint leaves, very finely chopped

Cut the scampi on the underside and, with the bony covering underneath, place in a shell. Sprinkle with the soy sauce and 1 tsp. of the lemon juice and season with a little salt and pepper. Grease a dish with some of the butter and lay the scampi in this. Cook for 3 (3¼) minutes at 360 (330) watts. Turn the scampi after half the cooking time and bring the bottom ones to the top. • Put the scampi on warmed plates and keep warm. Reduce the cream for 3 (3½) minutes at 600 (500) watts. Stir small pads of the remaining butter into the cooking liquid and add the remaining lemon juice. Season the sauce with salt, pepper and cayenne pepper and cream. Pour over the scampi and sprinkle with mint.

Tip: Lemon balm can be substituted for the mint. Scampi with the abdominal shell removed is very good to eat. The flesh is easily pulled out.

Cuttlefish Salad

Very easy

360 calories per serving
Preparation time: 10 minutes
Cooking time: 25 (28) minutes

Serves: 4 people

14 oz. cuttlefish (squid or mollusks)
½ cup water
2½ tbs. lemon juice
Salt, pepper
6 tbs. olive oil
½ tsp. basil, freshly chopped
½ tsp. oregano, freshly chopped
½ cup salad leaves of your choice
2 tomatoes
6 black olives
2 cloves garlic
2 tbs. parsley, freshly chopped

Trim the cuttlefish (squid or mollusks) and cut the tentacles in 1¼ in. long pieces. Put in a dish with the water and 1 tbs. of the lemon juice and cook, covered, for 25 (28) minutes at 600 (500) watts. • Mix the remaining lemon juice with some salt and pepper. Add the olive oil, mix well, then mix in the basil and oregano. • Trim and wash the salad leaves. Wash and dry the tomatoes and cut in wedges. Cool the cuttlefish (squid) a little. When lukewarm, mix with ⅔ of the salad dressing. • Arrange the cuttlefish (squid) salad on plates and garnish with green salad, tomato wedges and olives. • Pour the remaining salad dressing over the green salad. Peel and finely chop the garlic, mix it with the parsley and sprinkle over the fish salad.

Tip: The salad garnish can be omitted and the fish decorated with a sprig of flat parsley.

Stuffed Squid (or Mollusks)

More difficult

500 calories per serving
Preparation time: 25 minutes
Cooking time: 39 (40¾) minutes

Serves: 2 people

½ leek
¼ cup mushrooms
4 green olives
4 medium-sized squid
1 tsp. thyme leaves
½ cup white wine
1 tbs. olive oil
1 slice stale white bread
Salt, pepper
1 cup cream

Trim the leek, wash and chop finely. Trim the mushrooms and dice finely. Pit and finely chop the olives. Trim the squid, place in a dish and cover with salted water. Cook, covered, for 30 minutes at 490 (500) watts. Then drain and cut off the tentacles to chop them finely. Cook the thyme, white wine and olive oil for 2 (2½) minutes at 600 (500) watts. • Break the bread into pieces, put in a small dish and pour boiling water over. Squeeze out the soaked bread and press with a fork. Add to it the leek, mushrooms, tentacles, olives, salt and pepper and cook, covered for 2 (2½) minutes at 600 (500) watts. • Fill the squid with this mixture and cook with 2-3 tbs. of the cooking liquid for 3 (3¼) minutes at 360 (330) watts. Then keep warm. • Reduce the cooking liquid with the cream by cooking for 2 (2½) minutes at 600 (500) watts. Season the sauce, serve on to plates and lay the squid on top.

Seafood Fricassée

More expensive

500 calories per serving
Preparation time: 15 minutes
Cooking time: 11½ (12½) minutes

Serves: 2 people

| 4 trimmed scallops |
| 7 oz. fish filets (e.g. flounder or sea perch or sole) |
| 2 tbs. white wine |
| Salt, pepper |
| 1 cup cream |
| 2 tbs. port or dry sherry |
| 3 tbs. butter |
| 2 oz. cooked, shelled prawns or shrimp |
| Cayenne pepper |
| ½ tbs. parsley |

Cut the scallops in half across, remove the roe and cut it in small pieces. Cut the fish filets into cubes. Cook all to-gether with the white wine and a little salt and pepper, covered, for 3 minutes at 490 (500) watts. Strain the resulting stock through a sieve into another dish and re-duce with the cream for 6 (6½) minutes at 600 (500) watts. Add the port or sherry and cook for 2 (2½) minutes at 600 (500) watts. • Mix in the butter in small pieces. Add the scallops, fish and cooked prawns or shrimp and heat for ½ minute at 490 (500) watts. Season the fricassée with cayenne pepper and sprinkle with the parsley.

Tip: Cooked prawns are used in this dish, to save time. They are universally available. Raw or deep frozen prawns could be used instead, of course, in which case they should either be cooked or thawed in the micro-wave oven.

Scallops with Garlic

Very easy, more expensive

210 calories per serving
Preparation time: 30 minutes
Cooking time: 11½ (13) minutes

Serves: 4 people

| 12 scallops |
| ¼ cup butter |
| Salt, pepper |
| 3 tbs. lemon juice |
| 2 cloves garlic |
| 2 tbs. finely chopped parsley |
| 2 tbs. mixed herbs, freshly chopped (chervil, chives, tarragon) |
| 1 tbs. Marsala |
| 1 tbs. white wine |
| 2 lemons |

Open the scallops. Take out the flesh and remove the roe. Cut the flesh in half across. • Heat a browning dish for 4 (4½) minutes at 600 (500) watts. Melt the butter in this. Bake the scallops in this for 1 (1¼) min-utes at 600 (500) watts. Then turn over and cook for an addi-tional 1 (1¼) minutes at 600 (500) watts. Season the scallops with salt and pepper, sprinkle with the lemon juice and take out of the dish. • Peel and press the garlic and steam in the dish with the parsley and the other herbs for 2 minutes at 490 (500) watts. Sprinkle with the Marsala and white wine and reduce for 3 (3½) minutes at 600 (500) watts. • Return the scallops to the dish, cover, and cook for ½ minute at 490 (500) watts. Season again with salt and pepper. • Halve the lemons, prick the cut side of each half with a fork and serve with the scallops. At the table, squeeze over the scallops.

Fish Curry

More difficult

480 calories per serving
Preparation time: 20 minutes
Cooking time: 13 (15¼) minutes

Serves: 2 people

14 oz. sea bass
1½ tbs. butter
Salt
1-2 shallots
1 tbs. curry powder
1 tbs. flour
1 tbs. white wine
6 tbs. cream
Cayenne pepper
1 banana
1 kiwi fruit

Cut the fish into ½ in. cubes. • Heat a browning dish for 2 (2½) minutes at 600 (500) watts. Melt 1 tbs. of the butter in the dish. Steam the fish in this, covered, for 1 minute at 490 (500) watts. Then take out and sprinkle with salt. • Peel and chop the shallots, put in the dish and steam for 2 minutes at 490 (500) watts. • Dust with the curry powder and some of the flour and bake for 1 minute, covered, at 490 (500) watts. Add the white wine and cream and cook for 3 (3½) minutes at 600 (500) watts. Season the sauce with cayenne pepper. • Add the fish cubes and heat for 1 (1¼) minutes at 600 (500) watts. Then keep warm. • Heat a browning dish for 2 (2½) minutes at 600 (500) watts and add the remaining butter. Cut the banana in half lengthwise, dust it with the remaining flour and bake for ½ (¾) minute at 600 (500) watts. Turn it over on to the unused side of the dish and bake for another ½ (¾) minute at 600 (500) watts. Peel the kiwi fruit and cut in slices. Garnish the fish curry with the fruit.

Sea Bass with Tomato Sauce

More expensive

290 calories per serving
Preparation time: 10 minutes
Cooking time: 14 (15¼) minutes

Serves: 2 people

1 tbs. butter
6 slices sea bass (each about 2 oz.)
1 onion
1 clove garlic
2 tbs. tomato purée
Salt, pepper
1 tbs. brandy
½ cup white wine
Pinch dried oregano
Cayenne pepper

Heat a browning dish for 3 (3½) minutes at 600 (500) watts. Melt the butter in this. Add the fish slices and cook, covered, for 1 minute at 490 (500) watts. Take out the fish. Peel and finely chop the onion and put in the dish. Steam covered, for 3 minutes at 490 (500) watts. • Grate the onion through a fine sieve and return to the dish. Peel and press the garlic, then add to the dish with the tomato purée. Mix well, season with salt and pepper and steam for 1 minute at 490 (500) watts. Add the brandy, white wine, oregano and cayenne pepper. Reduce the sauce by cooking for 5 (5½) minutes at 600 (500) watts. Add the fish slices and heat for 1 (1¼) minutes at 600 (500) watts.

Gilt-Head Bream with Garlic

An Italian speciality

710 calories per serving
Preparation time: 15 minutes
Cooking time: 16 (18½) minutes

Serves: 2 people

1 gilt-head bream or flounder or sole (about 1¾ lb.)	
Salt, pepper	
8 cloves garlic	
¼ cup olive oil	
1 tbs. butter	
2 tbs. freshly chopped parsley	

Scale the fish and remove its innards. Wash out the stomach cavity and pat dry with paper towels. Salt and pepper the inside of the fish. Peel and finely chop the garlic. • Heat a browning dish for 4 (4½) minutes at 600 (500) watts. Put 2 tbs. of the olive oil in the dish, lay the fish on top and bake for 2 (2½) minutes at 600 (500) watts on each side. Sprinkle with salt and pepper, cover and cook for 6 (6½) minutes at 360 (330) watts. • Take out the fish and keep in a warm place. • Add the remaining olive oil and the butter to the dish with the garlic and parsley. Steam this mixture for 2 (2½) minutes at 600 (500) watts, season and pour over the fish.

Variations: Red mullet or gurnard (1 fish per person) look particularly attractive with this green garnish. Be careful, however, to scale these fish carefully without damaging the skin, otherwise the lovely red color is lost. Skinned, cored and finely diced tomatoes can be cooked with this dish, and instead of the garlic and parsley mixture, use finely chopped basil steamed with the fish in the final stages.

Giant Prawns on Zucchini

Very easy

330 calories per serving
Preparation time: 25 minutes
Cooking time: 6 minutes

Serves: 2 people

3 small zucchini
½ green pepper
1 shallot
Salt
1 tbs. butter
1 tbs. white wine
1 clove garlic
1 tsp. olive oil
6 giant prawns (shrimp) or scampi
Pepper

Wash and trim the zucchini. Cut in half lengthwise (do not peel) and scoop out the flesh. Chop the scooped out flesh. Wash, core and chop the pepper. Peel and chop the shallot and mix with the zucchini flesh and green pepper. Season with a little salt and divide between the zucchini shells. Grease a shallow dish with the butter and place the zucchini in this. Pour over the white wine. Peel and press the garlic and add to the zucchini with the olive oil. Shell the prawns (shrimp) or scampi and remove the intestine (brown threads). Cut in small pieces and lay on the zucchini. Sprinkle with a little pepper and cook, covered, for 6 minutes at 490 (500) watts.

Tip: If you do not wish to use green peppers, the mixture should be flavored with another spicy ingredient, such as cayenne pepper, soy sauce or dill.

Scampi with Melon Sauce

More difficult

480 calories per serving
Preparation time: 15 minutes
Cooking time: 6 (6½) minutes

Serves: 2 people

8 scampi
1 tbs. white wine
2 tbs. butter
1 small Ogen melon
¼ cup cream
Salt, pepper
Pinch cayenne pepper

Peel the scampi and put in a dish with the white wine and 1 tsp. of the butter. Cover and cook for 3 (3¼) minutes at 360 (330) watts. • Halve and de-seed the melon. Remove the flesh with a melon baller or spoon. Reserve a few balls for the sauce. • Pour off the cooking liquid from the scampi and purée in a mixer with the melon flesh. • Put the cream in a small dish and cook for 1 minute at 490 (500) watts. Add the melon purée and cook the sauce for 1 (1¼) minutes at 600 (500) watts. Season the sauce well with salt, pepper and cayenne pepper. Cut the remaining butter in small pads, add to the sauce with the scampi and reserved melon balls and finish cooking for 1 minute at 490 (500) watts.

Tip: If using deep-frozen scampi, use the defrost cycle for 7-8 minutes to thaw them. Then leave for 10 minutes before using.

Spaghetti with Shellfish

An Italian speciality

600 calories per serving
Preparation time: 15 minutes
Cooking time: 6 (6½) minutes

Serves: 2 people

1 cup spaghetti
Salt
14 oz. cleaned clams or carpet shells (vongole)
1 tbs. white wine
Pepper
½ bunch basil
1 small red pepper
1 cup cream

Put the spaghetti in rapidly boiling salted water and cook "al dente." Cook the shellfish, covered, with the white wine, a little salt and pepper for 4 minutes at 490 (500) watts. Wash and finely chop the basil.

Wash, trim and finely chop the red pepper, and add to the shells with the basil and cream. Reduce the sauce by cooking for 2 (2½) minutes at 600 (500) watts. Season with a little salt and pepper. Drain the cooked spaghetti and mix with the shellfish sauce.

Tip: If the sauce is too thick, thin it with 1-2 tbs. of the spaghetti cooking water. The pasta quickly soaks up the liquid. The pasta could also be cooked in the microwave oven (see following recipe), but this does not save any time. • Normally in Italy, the shells are mixed into the spaghetti, but if desired one or both halves of the shells can be removed in advanced. In this case, separate portions of the spaghetti should be heated in the microwave oven after mixing in the fish.

Pasta with Salmon Sauce

Very easy

670 calories per serving
Preparation time: 15 minutes
Cooking time: 13 (14½) minute

Serves: 2 people

Salt
¾ cup tagliatelle
2 tbs. butter
7 oz. fresh salmon
3 tbs. cream
Pepper
1 tbs. chervil, freshly chopped

Put 2 cups water and a little salt in a 3 cup capacity dish. Cover and bring to boil for 4 (4½) minutes at 600 (500) watts. Add the pasta and cook, without a lid, for 7 (8) minutes at 600 (500) watts. Drain, put in a warmed dish, mix with the butter and keep warm. • Finely dice the salmon. Purée 2 tbs. of the salmon with the cream. Stir the purée and diced salmon into the pasta and cook for 2 minutes at 490 (500) watts. Season with salt and pepper, and serve sprinkled with the chervil.

Tip: If you prefer a strong flavor, this dish can also be prepared with smoked salmon. In this case, however, only use 1 cup and do not purée any of it.

Variations: Instead of chervil, fine strips of leek can be added as a garnish. The pasta also tastes good with angler (monk) fish, prawns (shrimp) or mussels (clams).

Meat and Poultry

The microwave oven can be used to excellent effect in the preparation of meat and poultry dishes, combined with delicate sauces or other aromatic ingredients such as mushrooms or vegetables. For instance, the coq au vin in the picture has a wonderful flavor (recipe on page 81). Even a few tender pieces of meat can be transformed into a sustaining stew in the microwave oven. Roast beef, tender and pink in the middle, succeeds amazingly well too.

Above all, the microwave oven is of special interest to small households in the preparation of meat and poultry. It is possible to prepare a meat speciality for one or two people which would normally only be suitable for larger numbers.

Neither small nor large pieces of meat become crisp in the microwave oven. If you do not wish to miss out on this, a roast can be sealed in the oven in the normal way and then finished off for a short time in the microwave oven. A combination oven can be switched at will from broiler to convection or microwave.

Chopped Veal

Very easy, more expensive

400 calories per serving
Preparation time: 15 minutes
Cooking time: 10 (11¾) minutes
Serves: 2 people

10 oz. veal (loin)
1 onion
1 tbs. flour
3 tbs. white wine
1 tbs. meat bouillon
½ cup cream
Salt, pepper
1 tbs. parsley, freshly chopped

First cut the veal in slices, then strips. Peel and finely chop the onion. • Heat a browning dish for 4 (4½) minutes at 600 (500) watts. Place the veal on one half of the dish and seal for 1 (1¼) minute at 600 (500) watts. Turn the meat over on to the other half of the dish, do not switch on the oven but leave the dish to roast in the oven for a moment. Take out the meat and keep in a warm place. • Add the onion to the meat juices. Cover and steam for 2 (2½) minutes at 600 (500) watts. Sprinkle with the flour and pour over the white wine. Add the bouillon and the cream. Cook for 3 (3½) minutes at 600 (500) watts. Mix the meat with the sauce and season with salt and pepper. Serve, sprinkled with parsley.

Tip: The meat should be cut in fine, evenly sized pieces and should not cook in the sauce, otherwise it will become tough. Chicken can be used instead of veal; ¼ lb. trimmed and finely chopped mushrooms can be added to enhance the flavor.

Ragout of Veal with Madeira Sauce

More difficult

450 calories per serving
Preparation time: 25 minutes
Cooking time: 46 (49) minutes
Serves: 2 people

⅔ cup mushrooms
1 clove garlic
2 tomatoes
14 oz. veal (shoulder)
1 tbs. clarified butter
Salt, pepper
12 pearl onions
1 tsp. tomato paste
6 tbs. white wine
1 small sprig lovage
6 tbs. meat bouillon
3 tbs. Madeira
Cayenne pepper
Pinch sugar

Wash, trim and finely slice the mushrooms. Peel and crush the garlic. Skin, core and finely dice the tomatoes. Cut the meat in 1¼ in. dice. • Heat a browning dish for 4 (4½) minutes at 600 (500) watts. Melt the clarified butter in this, then place the meat on one half of the dish. Cook for 2 (2½) minutes at 600 (500) watts, turning the meat over on to the other half of the dish after half the cooking time. Season with salt and pepper. Add the pearl onions, garlic, mushrooms, tomatoes, tomato paste, white wine, lovage, meat bouillon and Madeira. • Cook, covered, for 40 (42) minutes at 360 (330) watts. Season with cayenne pepper, sugar and, if necessary, a little salt.

Tip: This dish can be improved with the addition of 1-2 tbs. cream.

White Veal Stew

A French speciality

360 calories per serving
Preparation time: 25 minutes
Cooking time: 40 (41¼) minutes)

Serves: 2 people

1 onion	
2 cloves	
1 bay leaf	
10 oz. veal (shoulder)	
1 leek	
1 small piece celery root	
1 carrot	
¾ cup water or meat bouillon	
2 peppercorns	
1 tbs. butter	
2 tsp. flour	
3 tbs. cream	
Salt, pepper	

Peel and halve the onions. Use a clove to spike half a bay leaf onto each onion half. Cut the veal into 1 in. cubes. Trim, wash and coarsely chop the vegetables. • Boil the water or bouillon, covered, with the onion, vegetables and crushed peppercorns for 5 (5½) minutes at 600 (500) watts. Add the meat and cook, covered, for 20 minutes at 490 (500) watts. Then cook for another 10 (10½) minutes at 360 (330) watts. • Remove the meat from the dish and keep warm. Strain the cooking liquid through a sieve and keep. • Melt the butter in a small dish for 1 (1¼) minutes at 600 (500) watts. Add the flour and stir well. Pour the bouillon on this and stir well again. Cook the sauce for 3 minutes at 490 (500) watts. Add the cream, season with salt and pepper and cook for 1 minute at 490 (500) watts. Mix with the meat.

Veal Stew with Vermouth Sauce

Very easy, more expensive

500 calories per serving
Preparation time: 15 minutes
Cooking time: 51 (54½) minutes

Serves: 2 people

14 oz. veal (shoulder)	
1 tbs. clarified butter	
Salt, pepper	
1 clove garlic	
1 tsp. tomato paste	
2 sage leaves	
½ cup meat bouillon	
¼ cup dry vermouth	
Pinch saffron powder	
6 tbs. cream	
Pinch sugar	
1 tsp. freshly chopped sage	
1 tsp. freshly chopped parsley	

Cut the veal into evenly sized cubes. • Heat a browning dish for 6 (6½) minutes at 600 (500) watts. Add the clarified butter and the meat and roast for 3 (3½) minutes at 600 (500) watts. Turn the meat over and season with salt and pepper. • Peel and crush the garlic and add to the meat with the tomato paste, sage leaves, meat bouillon and 2 tbs. of the vermouth. Cover and cook for 40 (42) minutes at 360 (330) watts. • Mix in the remaining vermouth, saffron and cream. Cook for 2 (2½) minutes at 600 (500) watts. Season the sauce with salt, pepper and sugar. Serve the stew sprinkled with the herbs.

Tip: The stew will have a stronger color if the diced meat is browned briefly in a skillet and then finished with the remaining ingredients as described.

Knuckle of Veal with Orange Sauce

More difficult

360 calories per serving
Preparation time: 10 minutes
Cooking time: 49 (52) minutes

Serves: 2 people

1 tbs. clarified butter
2 slices veal knuckle, each about 9 oz.
1 small carrot
1 onion
Salt, pepper
6 tbs. orange juice
½ tsp. grated orange rind
6 tbs. white wine
1 tsp. lemon juice
2 pinches meat extract or gravy granules
1 clove garlic
1 tsp. parsley, freshly chopped

Heat a browning dish for 6 (6½) minutes at 600 (500) watts. Place the clarified butter and slices of meat on one half of the dish and roast for 3 (3½) minutes at 600 (500) watts. Turn the meat over on to the other half of the dish and cook out of the oven for a moment. • Trim, wash and finely dice the carrot. Peel and finely chop the onion. Sprinkle both over the meat. Season with salt and pepper. Add the orange juice, orange rind, white wine, lemon juice and meat extract or gravy granules. Peel and crush the garlic and add to the mixture. • Cook the meat for 40 (42) minutes at 360 (330) watts. Season the sauce. Serve the meat sprinkled with the parsley.

Knuckle of Veal with Herb Sauce

More expensive

290 calories per serving
Preparation time: 10 minutes
Cooking time: 44 (46½) minutes

Serves: 2 people

2 slices knuckle of veal (each 9 oz.)
Salt, pepper
1 medium onion
1 tsp. butter
6 tbs. white wine
1 tsp. cornstarch
6 tbs. meat bouillon
1 clove garlic
2 tbs. mixed herbs (rosemary, basil, marjoram, thyme, parsley), freshly chopped
1 tsp. parsley, freshly chopped

Place the veal slices in a suitable dish. Sprinkle with salt and pepper. Peel and finely chop the onion and add to the meat with the butter. Cook, covered, for 4 (4½) minutes at 600 (500) watts. • Mix the white wine with the cornstarch. Stir in the meat bouillon and pour the mixture over the meat. Peel and crush the garlic and spread on top of the meat with the mixed herbs. Cook the meat, covered, for 40 (42) minutes at 360 (330) watts. Sprinkle with the chopped parsley.

Variations: This dish can be varied in many ways: add 2-3 tbs. cream and heat for 2 (2½) minutes at 600 (500) watts; or halve a peeled tomato, core and finely dice it and add to the meat after cooking, then heat for 2 (2½) minutes at 600 (500) watts.

Veal Steak with Pate De Foie Gras

An indulgence, more expensive

600 calories per serving
Preparation time: 20 minutes
Cooking time: 13 (15¼) minutes

Serves: 2 people

2 veal steaks, each about 6 oz.
2 thin slices pâté de foie gras
Salt, pepper
A little flour
1 tbs. clarified butter
1 shallot or small onion
2 tbs. whisky
½ cup cream

Heat a large browning dish for 4 (4½) minutes at 600 (500) watts. Beat the steaks flat and cut into one side to create a pocket. Push into each pocket one slice of pâté de foie gras and close with toothpicks. Sprinkle with salt and pepper and a little flour. • Place the meat with the clarified butter in the browning dish and press down a little. Cook for 2 (2½) minutes at 600 (500) watts, then turn the steaks over on to the unused half of the dish. Cook for an additional 2 (2½) minutes at 600 (500) watts. Take out the meat and keep warm. • Peel and chop the onion or shallot and steam in the cooking juices for 1 (1¼) minutes at 600 (500) watts. Add the whisky and cream. Reduce the sauce for 4 (4½) minutes at 600 (500) watts. Serve the sauce separately with the steaks.

Tip: Some thyme leaves can be added to the filling and the steaks garnished with a sprig of thyme. Do not forget to remove the toothpicks before serving.

Tenderloin of Veal with Mushrooms

More difficult

240 calories per serving
Preparation time: 20 minutes
Cooking time: 15 (17) minutes

Serves: 4 people

½ cup mushrooms
2 cloves garlic
1 tbs. butter at room temperature
Pinch paprika powder
1 tbs. sharp mustard
1 tsp. thyme leaves
1 lb. 2 oz. veal tenderloin
Salt, pepper
1 tbs. white wine
6 tbs. cream

Trim and quarter the mushrooms. Peel and crush the garlic. Heat a browning dish for 4 (4½) minutes at 600 (500) watts. Mix the butter well with the garlic, paprika powder, mustard and thyme. Spread this mixture on the tenderloin. Place the meat on one half of the browning dish. Cook for 3 (3½) minutes at 600 (500) watts, then turn over on to the other half of the dish and cook for an additional 3 (3½) minutes at 600 (500) watts. Sprinkle salt and pepper all over the meat, take out of the dish and put on a heated plate, cover with foil and keep warm. • Mix the white wine with the meat juices. Add the cream and mushrooms and cook for 5 (5½) minutes at 600 (500) watts. Cut the meat in ¾ in. thick slices, spoon the mushrooms over it and pour over the sauce.

Tip: Garnish the dish with a little thyme and halved, steamed cherry tomatoes.

Boeuf Bourguignonne

More difficult

810 calories per serving
Preparation time: 20 minutes
Cooking time: 70 (74) minutes

Serves: 2 people

14 oz. chuck
2 oz. smoked bacon
1 tbs. clarified butter
Salt, pepper
1 large carrot
10 pearl onions
1 clove garlic
½ tbs. thyme leaves
1 bay leaf
1 tbs. tomato paste
1 piece orange rind
1 sprig lovage
1¼ cups red wine
6 tbs. meat bouillon
1 tsp. cornstarch

Cut the meat into 1¼ in. cubes. Dice the bacon. Heat a browning dish for 6 (6½) minutes at 600 (500) watts. Place the clarified butter, meat and diced bacon on one half of the dish. Roast for 4 (4½) minutes at 600 (500) watts. Turn the meat over on to the other half of the dish, switch off the oven and cook the meat briefly in the oven. Sprinkle with salt and pepper. • Peel, wash and finely slice the carrot. Peel and crush the garlic. Add the carrot, onions, garlic, thyme, bay leaf, tomato paste, orange rind, lovage and the red wine to the meat. Mix the meat bouillon with the cornstarch and stir into the meat. Cover and cook the meat for 60 (63) minutes at 360 (330) watts.

Carbonade or Beef with Green Pepper

Very easy

500 calories per serving
Preparation time: 5 minutes
Cooking time: 41 (43¾) minutes

Serves: 2 people

1½ tbs. butter
4 thin slices beef (chuck or flank), each 3 oz.
Salt, pepper
1 shallot
2 cloves garlic
½ tbs. flour
⅔ cup dark beer
6 tbs. meat bouillon
1 tsp. green peppercorns in brine
1 tsp. tomato paste
Grated nutmeg
½ tsp. thyme leaves

Heat a browning dish for 6 (6½) minutes at 600 (500) watts. Melt 1 tbs. of the butter in the dish, add the meat slices and cook for 4 (4½) minutes at 600 (500) watts. Turn the meat over and cook for a few minutes out of the oven. Sprinkle with salt and pepper. • Peel and finely chop the onion and garlic and put on top of the meat. Cover and steam for 1 (1¼) minute at 600 (500) watts. Dust the meat with the flour and pour over the beer. Add the meat bouillon, green peppercorns, tomato paste, a little nutmeg and the thyme. • Cover and cook for 30 (31½) minutes at 360 (330) watts. Stir the remaining butter, cut in small pieces, into the sauce.

Tip: The browning process is more successful when done in a special dish. If the meat is first placed on one half of the dish

and then turned over on to the unused half, the heat is used more efficiently.

Roast Beef

Very easy, more expensive

330 calories per serving
Preparation time: 10 minutes
Cooking time: 18 (20½) minutes

Serves: 6 people

Salt, pepper
1 tbs. sharp mustard
2¼ lbs. roasting beef
1 tbs. clarified butter

Mix a little salt and pepper with the mustard. Spread this mixture all over the beef. Heat a suitable browning dish for 4 (4½) minutes at 600 (500) watts. Add the clarified butter and let it melt. Place the meat on one half of the dish. Roast for 7

(8) minutes at 600 (500) watts. Turn the meat over on to the unused part of the dish and cook for an additional 7 (8) minutes at 600 (500) watts. Remove the meat from the oven, wrap in tinfoil and leave to rest for 5-10 minutes. This prevents the meat juices from coming out of the meat when it is sliced.

Tip: While the meat is resting, you could prepare a Béarnaise sauce from the recipe on page 39, using the microwave oven.

Plate Meal with Vegetables

Very easy, good value

480 calories per serving
Preparation time: 20 minutes
Cooking time: 59 (62) minutes

Serves: 2 people

10 oz. boiling beef (chuck or brisket)
1 leek
1 large carrot
1 small piece celery root
2 cups water
1 tsp. gravy granules
½ bay leaf
2-3 parsley stalks
Pepper
2 slices beef marrow bones

Cut the meat in large cubes. Trim and wash the vegetables and cut in large pieces or cubes. • Boil the water, gravy

granules, bay leaf, parsley stalks and a little pepper in a dish for 5 (5½) minutes at 600 (500) watts. Add the meat and vegetables. Cover and cook for 50 (52½) minutes at 360 (330) watts. • Meanwhile, put the marrow bones in cold water. Drain well, add to the dish and cook for an additional 4 minutes at 490 (500) watts.

Tip: If you prefer your vegetables crunchy, add them 10 minutes before the end of the cooking time. The exact time required for cooking the meat depends on the quality. You can use, for example, a piece of rump which is normally used for roasting, in which case the cooking time is reduced by a third. For best results, test the meat before serving and if it is not oven tender, return to the microwave over for a short time.

Ham Steaks with Madeira Sauce

Very quick

500 calories per serving
Cooking time: 12 (13½) minutes

Serves: 2 people

1 tbs. clarified butter
2 slices ham (¼-½ in. thick)
6 tbs. Madeira
Pinch onion powder
1 tbs. tomato ketchup
Salt, pepper
1 tsp. parsley, freshly chopped

Heat a browning dish with the clarified butter for 6 (6½) minutes at 600 (500) watts. Lay the ham slices in the dish and cook, without turning, for 2 (2½) minutes at 600 (500) watts. Put the ham on warmed plates and keep warm. • Pour the Madeira into the dish. Add the onion powder and ketchup and stir well. Reduce for 4 (4½) minutes at 600 (500) watts. Season the sauce with salt and pepper. Pour over the steaks and serve sprinkles with parsley.

Tip: If you prefer a stronger sauce, add a little cayenne pepper. Mashed potatoes, prepared as in the recipe on page 45, go well with the ham steaks. A few sage leaves can be cooked with the steaks. The Madeira can be substituted by Marsala or red wine. Dried prunes go particularly well with the red wine.

Ragoût of Pork with Prunes

More difficult

1305 calories per serving
Preparation time: 15 minutes
Cooking time: 61 (65) minutes

Serves: 2 people

14 oz. pork (shoulder)
2 oz. smoked bacon
1 onion
1 tbs. clarified butter
Salt, pepper
2 tbs. butter
1 cup dark beer
1 small carrot
¾ cup prunes
1 clove
1 sprig thyme
1 tsp. cornstarch
½ cup meat bouillon

Cut the meat into large cubes. Dice the bacon. Peel and finely chop the onion. • Heat a browning dish for 5 (5½) minutes at 600 (500) watts. Put the clarified butter, meat and bacon on one half of the dish. Cook for 4 (4½) minutes at 600 (500) watts. Turn over on to the other half of the dish and continue to cook outside the oven. Season with salt and pepper. • Steam the onion with 1 tsp. of the butter in a small dish for 2 (2½) minutes at 600 (500) watts. Pour the beer over it. Pour this mixture over the beef. Trim, wash and slice the carrot. Add to the meat with the dried prunes, clove and thyme. Stir the cornstarch into the meat bouillon and add to the meat. • Cover and cook the ragoût for 50 (52½) minutes at 360 (330) watts. Stir the remaining butter, cut into small pieces, into the sauce.

Crumbed Tarragon Steak

Very quick

480 calories per serving
Preparation time: 20 minutes
Cooking time: 6 (7¼) minutes

Serves: 2 people

2 pork or veal steaks, each 6 oz.
4-6 tarragon leaves
1 tbs. butter
Salt, pepper
½ tbs. flour
1 egg
½ cup breadcrumbs
2 tbs. clarified butter

Cut a pocket into a long side of each steak. Wash and coarsely chop the tarragon. Mix with the butter and fill each pocket with half of the mixture. • Sprinkle the steaks with salt and pepper and coat lightly with flour. Dip into the beaten egg and finally coat with breadcrumbs, pressing the breadcrumbs well on to the meat. Heat clarified butter in a large browning dish for 3 (3½) minutes at 600 (500) watts. • Place the steaks on one half of the dish and cook for 2 (2½) minutes at 600 (500) watts. Turn the meat over on to the other half of the dish and cook for an additional 1 (1¼) minute at 600 (500) watts.

Tip: The steaks can be garnished with a lemon wedge and tarragon.

Variations: Fill the steaks with a thin slice of tomato and cheese. Or fill each with a slice of raw ham and 1 sage leaf.

Lamb Cutlets Provencale

Very quick

640 calories per serving
Preparation time: 15 minutes
Cooking time: 7 (8) minutes

Serves: 2 people

2 cloves garlic
1 small onion
1 tbs. mixed herbs (basil, marjoram, thyme, savory, sage, parsley), freshly chopped, or 1 tsp. provençale herb mixture
1 tbs. butter at room temperature
Salt, pepper
4 lamb cutlets, each 3 oz.

Peel and finely chop the garlic and onion and mix well with the herbs and butter. Season with salt and pepper. Heat a browning dish for 5 (5½) minutes at 600 (500) watts. Spread the butter mixture on both sides of the lamb cutlets. Put the meat on the heated dish and cook on both sides for 1 (1¼) minutes at 600 (500) watts on each side.

Tip: Serve the cutlets immediately and do not reheat, or they will become moist. This dish can also be prepared with pork cutlets.

Liver in Vinegar

Good value

450 calories per serving
Preparation time: 10 minutes
Cooking time: 8 (9¾) minutes

Serves: 2 people

14 oz. pig's liver
1 onion
1½ tbs. butter
Salt, pepper
3 tbs. red wine
1 tbs. wine vinegar
1 tbs. tomato ketchup
1 tbs. Madeira

Trim the liver and cut in thin slices. Peel and finely chop the onion. • Heat a browning dish for 4 (4½) minutes at 600 (500) watts. Melt about 1 tbs. of the butter in the dish, place the liver in it and cook for ½ (¾) minute at 600 (500) watts. Season the liver with salt and pep-per, cover with foil and put on one side. • Put the remaining butter in another browning dish. Add the onion and steam for 1 (1¼) minutes at 500 (500) watts. Pour over the red wine. Add the vinegar, ketchup and Madeira and mix well. Cook for 2 (2½) minutes at 600 (500) watts. Put the liver in the sauce and heat for ½ (¾) minute at 600 (500) watts. Season the sauce to taste.

Tip: Ox or calves' liver can be prepared the same way, although calves' liver is more expensive. The liver should only be salted after cooking, otherwise it will become tough.

Veal Sweetbreads with Apples

More difficult, more expensive

520 calories per serving
Soaking time: 1 hour
Preparation time: 20 minutes
Cooking time: 12 (13¾) minutes

Serves: 2 people

¾ lb. veal sweetbreads
1 onion
Salt, white pepper
1½ tbs. butter
1 small apple
1 tbs. Calvados
½ cup cream
Pinch cayenne pepper
1 tsp. chervil, freshly chopped

Soak the sweetbreads in cold water for 1 hour. Peel away the cartilage, fibers and remove any dirt. Peel and chop the onion. • Heat a browning dish for 4 (4½) minutes at 600 (500) watts. Cut the sweetbreads in 4 slices. Place on one half of the dish and cook for 2 (2½) minutes at 600 (500) watts. Sprinkle the slices with salt and pepper and turn over on to the other half of the dish. After about 1 minute, remove the meat from the plate and keep warm. • Put the butter on the warm dish. Add the onion and cook for 1 minute at 490 (500) watts. Pour over the Calvados and add the cream. Reduce the sauce for 4 (4½) minutes at 600 (500) watts. Season with salt, pepper and cayenne pepper. Divide the sauce between 2 warmed plates and top each with 2 slices of sweetbreads. Serve sprinkled with chervil.

Tripe with Mustard Sauce

Very easy, good value

405 calories per serving
Resting time: 1 hour
Preparation time: 20 minutes
Cooking time: 33 (38) minutes

Serves: 2 people

¾ lb. tripe, cooked by the butcher

1 onion

1 bay leaf

1 clove

1 leek

¼ cup meat bouillon

2 tbs. butter

½ tbs. flour

1 tbs. sharp mustard

4-6 tbs. cream

Salt, pepper

S oak the tripe in cold water for 1 hour. Drain well and cut in thin strips. Peel the onion and use the clove to spike the bay leaf on to it. Trim the leek then cut off the ends. Put the end pieces of onion, leek, meat bouillon and tripe in a dish and cook, covered, for 15 (17) minutes at 600 (500) watts. • Cut the remaining leek in thin slices. Put in a small dish with the butter, cover, and cook for 4 (4½) minutes at 600 (500) watts. • Meanwhile, allow the tripe to continue cooking in the covered dish in the oven at the sauce time. Dust the leek with the flour, add 1 cup cooking liquid from the tripe and cook the sauce, covered for 10 (11½) minutes at 600 (500) watts. Add the mustard, then the drained tripe, mix well and cook, covered, for 2 (2½) minutes at 600 (500) watts. Stir in the cream and heat, uncovered, for 2 (2½) minutes at 600 (500) watts. Season with salt and pepper.

Tripe with Herbs

Very easy

314 calories per serving
Soaking time: 1 hour
Preparation time: 25 minutes
Cooking time: 25 (27) minutes

Serves: 2 people

¾ lb. tripe, cooked by the butcher

1 tomato

1 onion

1 tbs. olive oil or butter

1 clove garlic

1 tsp. tomato paste

5-6 peppercorns

2 tbs. freshly chopped mixed herbs (basil, marjoram, thyme, savory)

1 bay leaf

6 tbs. red wine

1 cup meat bouillon

Salt, pepper

1 tbs. breadcrumbs

1 tbs. parsley, freshly chopped

1 tbs. butter

S oak the tripe in cold water for 1 hour. Meanwhile, skin and finely dice the tomato. Peel and chop the onion and put it in a dish with the tomato and olive oil or butter and cook for 3 (3½) minutes at 600 (500) watts. • Cut the tripe in 1¼ in. cubes. Peel and crush the garlic and add to the tripe with the tomato paste. Mix well with the tomato and onion. Crush the peppercorns and add to the tripe with the herbs, bay leaf, red wine and meat bouillon and cook, covered, for 20 (21) minutes at 360 (330) watts. Season the dish with salt and pepper. • Mix the breadcrumbs with the parsely and sprinkle on the tripe. Top with the butter, cut in small pieces, and heat for 2 (2½) minutes at 600 (500) watts.

Chicken Fricassé with Vegetables

Very easy

200 calories per serving
Preparation time: 25 minutes
Cooking time: 14 (16) minutes

Serves: 4 people

1 small carrot
1 small green pepper
½ cup celery
1 small kohlrabi
½ cup meat bouillon
1 small zucchini
¼ cup mushrooms
2 shallots
1 lb. 2 oz. chicken breasts (skinned and boned)
½ cup hot water
2 tbs. instant gravy
½ cup white wine
Salt, pepper
½ tsp. thyme

Trim and wash the carrot, green pepper, celery and kohlrabi and cut in fine slices. Put in a dish with the meat bouillon and cook, covered, for 3 (3½) minutes at 600 (500) watts. Wash, trim, and finely slice the zucchini and mushrooms. Peel and finely chop the shallots and add with the zucchini and mushrooms to the cooked vegetables. Cover and cook for 4 (4½) minutes at 600 (500) watts. • Cut the chicken breasts into bite-sized pieces, add to the vegetables and cook, covered, for 2 (2½) minutes at 600 (500) watts. Continue the cooking process in the covered dish. Stir in the instant gravy and white wine into the hot water. Reduce in a small dish for 5 (5½) minutes at 600 (500) watts. Mix the sauce into the meat and vegetables. Season with salt, pepper and thyme.

Chicken with Champagne Sauce

More difficult, more expensive

550 calories per serving
Preparation time: 30 minutes
Cooking time: 21 (23¾) minutes

Serves: 4 people

1 carrot
1 shallot
1 chicken (about 3 lbs.)
1 tbs. butter
Salt, pepper
1 miniature bottle champagne (4 oz.)
1 bay leaf
6 tbs. cream
½ tsp. cornstarch
½ cup cold butter

Trim, wash and very finely dice the carrot. Peel and chop the shallot. Cut the chicken into 8 pieces, then skin them. • Put in a suitable dish with the butter and shallot. Cover and cook for 4 (4½) minutes at 600 (500) watts. Season with salt and pepper, add half the champagne, the carrot and the bay leaf. Cook the chicken pieces for 5 (5¼) minutes, covered, at 360 (330) watts. Then take them out of the dish and cover with foil. Stir the cream with the cornstarch. Add to the cooking juices from the chicken and reduce for 10 (11½) minutes at 600 (500) watts. Stir in the remaining champagne. Return the chicken pieces to the dish, cover, and cook for 2 (2½) minutes at 600 (500) watts. • Arrange the meat on plates, remove the bay leaf from the sauce and stir in the butter, cut in small pieces.

Coq Au Vin

A French Speciality

790 calories per serving
Preparation time: 30 minutes
Cooking time: 42 (47) minutes

Serves: 3 people

1 chicken (2¼-2½ lbs)

2 oz. smoked bacon

2 tbs. clarified butter

12 pearl onions

Salt, pepper

Pinch sugar

1 clove garlic

1 bay leaf

¾ cup mushrooms

1 small piece celery root

1 small carrot

1 tsp. marjoram, freshly chopped

2 cups red wine

½ cup chicken bouillon

2-3 tsp. cornstarch

1 tbs. parsley, freshly chopped

Skin the chicken and cut into 12 pieces. Dice the bacon. Heat a browning dish with the clarified butter for 5 (5½) minutes at 600 (500) watts. • Add the chicken pieces and bacon and cook for 4 (4½) minutes at 600 (500) watts, turn over, add the onion and leave for a few minutes. Season the meat with salt, pepper and sugar. Peel and crush the garlic and add to the meat with the bay leaf. Trim and quarter the mushrooms. Trim, wash and finely dice the celery root and carrot. Mix into the chicken with the marjoram. Pour over about 1½ cups red wine and the chicken bouillon. Cover and cook for 10 (10½) minutes at 360 (330) watts. Remove chicken from the dish and cover. • Stir the remaining red wine with the cornstarch. Add to the vegetables and reduce for 20 (23) minutes at 600 (500) watts. Return the chicken pieces to the dish and heat, covered, for 3 (3½) minutes at 600 (500) watts. Sprinkle with parsley and serve.

Ragout of Rabbit

Very easy

330 calories per serving
Preparation time: 15 minutes
Cooking time: 36 (37¾) minutes

Serves: 4 people

1 tbs. butter
2¼ lbs. rabbit, in 8 pieces
1 clove garlic
¼ cup tomato paste
1 green pepper
3 tbs. red wine
3 tbs. water
Salt, pepper
Pinch cayenne pepper

Heat a browning dish for 4 (4½) minutes at 600 (500) watts. Melt the butter in the dish. Add the meat and cook for 3 minutes at 490 (500) watts, stirring after half the cooking time. • Peel and crush the garlic and add to the meat with the tomato paste. Wash, trim and finely slice the green pepper and add to the meat. Pour in the red wine and water. Cover and cook for 25 (26¼) minutes at 360 (330) watts. Take out the meat. • Reduce the sauce for 4 minutes at 490 (500) watts, then add salt, pepper and cayenne pepper to taste. Pour the sauce over the meat.

Spicy Peppered Venison

More difficult, more expensive

220 calories per serving
Preparation time: 30 minutes
Marinating time: 3-5 days
Cooking time: 69 (73¼) minutes

Serves: 4 people

14 oz. boned haunch of venison
1 carrot
1 piece celery root
1 leek
2 shallots
6 juniper berries
½ bay leaf
1 tsp. black peppercorns
3 tbs. red wine vinegar
1 cup red wine
Salt, pepper
1 tsp. thyme
3 tbs. venison or pig blood
3 tbs. cream
1 tsp. cornstarch

Cut the venison into 1¼ in. cubes. • For the marinade, peel or trim, wash and finely chop the carrot, celery root, leek and the shallots. Mix with the crushed juniper berries, bay leaf, peppercorns, vinegar and red wine. Pour over the meat, cover and leave to marinade in the refrigerator for 3-5 days. • Remove the meat from the marinade and pat dry. Heat a browning dish for 4 (4½) minutes at 600 (500) watts. Add the meat and cook for 4 (4½) minutes at 600 (500) watts. Turn the meat over. • Strain the marinade through a sieve and season the liquid with salt, pepper and thyme. Add to the meat, cover and cook for 60 (63) minutes at 360 (330) watts. Remove the meat from the sauce. Strain the sauce. Stir the blood into the cream and cornstarch and add to the sauce. Return to the dish with the meat and heat for 1 (1¼) minute at 600 (500) watts.

Tip: Remember to order the blood in good time.

Saddle of Hare with Grapes

More expensive

330 calories per serving
Preparation time: 35 minutes
Marinating time: 24 hours
Cooking time: 13 (14½) minutes

Serves: 4 people

1¾ lbs. saddle of hare
2 sprigs rosemary
1 carrot
1 small piece celery root
½ leek
1 small onion
6 juniper berries
1 bay leaf
8 black peppercorns
2 tbs. red wine vinegar
1¼ cups red wine
1 tbs. butter
1 shallot
¼ lb. grapes
½ tsp. tomato paste
1 tbs. cornstarch
Salt, pepper

Ease the meat away from the backbone with a spoon, then cut half-way through. Stick a sprig of rosemary in each side. Place in a dish. • For the marinade, peel or trim the vegetables and the onion and cut them in small pieces. Mix with the crushed juniper berries, bay leaf, peppercorns, vinegar and red wine and pour over the meat. Cover with foil and leave to marinate in the refrigerator for 24 hours. • Then heat a browning dish for 4 (4½) minutes at 600 (500) watts. Remove the meat from the marinade and pat dry with a paper towel. Melt the butter in the browning dish. Place the meat in the dish with the meat side underneath. Cook for 4 (4½) minutes at 600 (500) watts, turning the meat over after half the cooking time. Remove the meat. Peel and chop the shallot. • Steam the grapes and shallot on the hot plate for 2 (2½) minutes at 600 (500) watts. Add the tomato paste. Stir half of the marinade into the cornstarch and mix in. Return the meat to the dish, cover and cook for 3 minutes at 490 (500) watts. Take out the meat and wrap in foil, so that it remains warm. • Strain the sauce through a sieve, season and serve separately with the meat.

Tip: The sauce can be improved by adding 1-2 tbs. cream. When carving the meat, carefully detach it from the bones using the back of a spoon, then cut in slanting ¾ in. thick slices. Lay the meat back on the bones and recreate its original shape. Noodles, chestnut purée and red cabbage go well with this dish.

Variations: The grapes can be omitted and substituted with prunes puréed with a little prune juice and added to the sauce. Or replace the grapes with lightly caramelized apple slices and season the sauce with a little Calvados. This dish can be cooked more quickly by easing the raw meat from the bones, cutting it in slices and cooking the slices on the browning dish. Chop the bones in pieces and make a game sauce with finely chopped vegetables and red wine.

Chicken Kebabs

Good value

160 calories per serving
Preparation time: 15 minutes
Cooking time: 2 (2½) minute
Serves: 2 people

2 shallots
4 small mushrooms
1 chicken breast (boned)
1 small zucchini
1 tsp. olive oil
Salt, pepper, paprika powder
1 tsp. rosemary freshly chopped

Peel and halve the shallots. Trim and wash the mushrooms thoroughly. Cut the meat in 1¼ in. cubes. Trim and wash the zucchini and cut in 1¼ in. thick slices. Thread all these ingredients, alternately, on to 4 skewers. Brush with olive oil and sprinkle with salt, pepper, paprika and rosemary. Cook the

kebabs for 2 (2½) minutes at 600 (500) watts.

Tip: Cumin gives the kebabs an interesting flavor.

Variations: Substitute an eggplant for the zucchini in which case steam the eggplant slices with 1 tsp. oil and 1 tbs. water for 1 minute at 490 (500) watts before threading onto skewer with the other ingredients. Alternatively, halve, core, wash, then quarter a green pepper, steam it and then thread on to the skewer with the other ingredients.

Chicken with Caper Sauce

Very easy

450 calories per serving
Preparation time: 20 minutes
Cooking time: 22 (24¾) minute
Serves: 4 people

1 chicken (2¼-2½) lbs.
1-2 shallots
1 tbs. butter
Salt, pepper
⅔ cup white wine
2 tsp. cornstarch
⅔ cup chicken bouillon
½ cup cream
1-2 tbs. capers

Skin the chicken and cut in 8 pieces. Peel and chop the shallots. Put the chicken pieces in a suitable dish with the butter and shallots. Cover and cook for 4 (4½) minutes at 600 (500)

watts. Sprinkle with salt and pepper. Pour over the white wine. Stir the cornstarch into the chicken bouillon and add to the dish. • Cook for 5 (5¼) minutes at 360 (330) watts, covered. Then take out the chicken pieces and keep warm. Add the cream to the sauce, stir well and reduce for 10 (11½) minutes at 600 (500) watts. Return the meat to the sauce, add the capers, cover, and cook for 3 (3½) minutes at 600 (500) watts.

Tip: This dish can easily be prepared for 2 people (in this case buy chicken pieces). Reduce the cooking time by about half.

Variations: Replace the capers with a little chopped tarragon added at the end of the cooking process. Or make small carrot or zucchini balls which are cooked with the meat for 5 (5¼) minutes at 360 (330) watts.

Irish Stew

A British Specialty

570 calories per serving
Preparation time: 20 minutes
Cooking time: 41 (43) minutes

Serves: 4 people

2 cups meat bouillon
1 lb. 2 oz. lamb (shoulder)
2 onions
1 small piece celery root
1 carrot
2 large potatoes
Salt, pepper

Bring the stock to a boil by cooking for 7 (8) minutes at 600 (500) watts. • Heat a browning dish for 4 (4½) minutes at 600 (500) watts. Cut the meat in 1 in. cubes and cook for 2 (2½) minutes at 600 (500) watts. Turn the meat over and pour on the bouillon. Cover and cook for 8 minutes at 490 (500) watts.

Meanwhile, peel and finely slice the onions. Trim, wash and thickly slice the celery root, carrot and potatoes. Add to the meat with the onions, cover and cook for 20 minutes at 490 (500) watts. • Leave the covered dish to stand for 2 minutes, then season to taste with salt and pepper.

Pork Casserole

Very easy, good value

670 calories per serving
Preparation time: 30 minutes
Cooking time: 69 (70) minutes

Serves: 3 people

14 oz. pork (lean neck end)
1 small onion
1 leek
2 carrots
2¼ cups white cabbage or Savoy cabbage
¾ cup green beans
2 tbs. butter
½ tsp. dried marjoram
½ tsp. dried thyme
1¼ cups bouillon
Salt, pepper
Grated nutmeg
1¾ cup potatoes

Cut the meat in ¾ in. cubes. Peel and chop the onion. Trim and wash the leek and carrots, then slice them. Wash and halve the cabbage, remove the thick ribs and cut the leaves in strips. String, wash and halve the beans. Heat a large browning dish for 2 (2½) minutes at 600 (500) watts. Add the butter and meat and cook for 3 (3½) minutes at 600 (500) watts. Add the onion, cover, and steam for 4 minutes at 490 (500) watts. Add the vegetables, herbs and ¾ cup bouillon. Season with salt, pepper and nutmeg. Cover and cook for 45 minutes at 490 (500) watts. Peel, wash and finely dice the potatoes, and add to the meat. Cover and cook for 15 minutes at 490 (500) watts. Stir in the remaining meat bouillon.

Vegetables, Souffles, One-Pot Dishes

Vegetables cooked "al dente," as they have been in China for centuries, are becoming increasingly popular with connoisseurs. Using the microwave oven, vegetables can be carefully cooked in their own juices or with only a tiny bit of water. This method retains the fresh colors and the full flavors of the vegetables. In addition, the short cooking time means that hardly any vitamins and minerals are lost. They remain in precisely measured juices which can be used as they are or added to a delicate sauce to enhance its flavor. Microwave cooking is also healthy cooking. In this chapter, you will find not only delicious vegetable side dishes, but also complete main courses, one-pot dishes and delicious soufflés, which taste and look good. "Eggplants and tomatoes," illustrated here, are always popular. The recipe is on page 101.

Kohlrabi with Cheese

Very easy

220 calories per serving
Preparation time: 20 minutes
Cooking time: 10 (11½) minutes

Serves: 2 people

2 cups olive oil or butter
14 oz. kohlrabi
1 medium onion
Salt, pepper, grated nutmeg
2 tbs. Parmesan, freshly grated
⅔ cup vegetable or meat bouillon

Grease a shallow dish with the olive oil or butter. Peel the kohl rabi and cut in ⅛ in. slices. Peel and chop the onion. Arrange the kohl rabi in the dish in overlapping slices. Season each layer with a little salt, pepper, nutmeg, onion and Parmesan. Finish with kohl rabi, pour over the bouillon. Sprinkle with the remaining Parmesan. Cover and cook for 10 (11½) minutes at 600 (500) watts.

Tip: For best results, the kohl rabi should be sliced using a vegetable grater. When cooked as described above, the kohl rabi is still crisp. If you prefer it cooked a little more, you can interrupt the cooking process after 5 minutes and turn the kohl rabi over.

Variations: Tiny cubes of ham can be sprinkled over the kohl rabi instead of cheese. Or cut the kohl rabi in slightly thicker slices, pour over thick sour cream or fresh cream, sprinkle with grated nutmeg and heat for another 1 (1¼) minute at 600 (500) watts.

Cucumber in Mango Sauce

Delicious

130 calories per serving
Preparation time: 10 minutes
Cooking time: 7 (7¾) minutes

Serves: 2 people

1 medium cucumber
2 tbs. butter
Salt, pepper
3 oz. mango, weighted after peeling
½ tsp. soy sauce
Pinch cayenne pepper
1 tsp. lemon juice
6 tbs. water

Wash and trim the cucumber and cut into 2¼ in. lengths. Remove the core with an apple corer, then cut in ⅛ in. slices. Place the slices in a dish with the butter. Sprinkle with salt and pepper, cover and cook for 6 (6½) minutes at 600 (500) watts. • Meanwhile, prepare the sauce by peeling the mango and easing the fruit from the stone. Purée the mango with the soy sauce, cayenne pepper, lemon juice and water. Mix the purée into the cucumber. Cover and cook for 1 (1¼) minute at 600 (500) watts.

Tip: When buying, make sure the mango is ripe (soft), so that the sauce will have enough flavor.

Variations: Cook the cucumber rings as described above, cool, then mix with 1 small carton yogurt, 1 tbs. ground almonds and 3 crushed garlic cloves. Season with salt and pepper.

Asparagus

Very easy

65 calories per serving
Preparation time: 15 minutes
Cooking time: 8 (9) minutes

Serves: 2 people

2¼ cups asparagus
½ cup water
Pinch salt
Pinch sugar

Trim and wash the asparagus, cutting off the ends. Lay in a dish. Add the water, salt and sugar. Cover and cook for 8 (9) minutes at 600 (500) watts, turning the asparagus after half the cooking time. Leave covered for 2 minutes to finish cooking.

Tip: The cooking time of the asparagus depends on the quality, origin and thickness of the stalks. It is important, therefore, to test it before serving. If necessary, cook for an additional 1-2 minutes. (As a rule, do not peel green asparagus.) In this case, 14 oz. is enough for 2 people. The cooking time is the same as for white asparagus, but it should be left for 4 minutes after cooking.

Variations: The cooked asparagus can be reheated, topped with chopped, hard-boiled eggs, 1 tbs. parsley and 1 tbs. breadcrumbs and 3 tbs. butter for 1 (1¼) minute at 600 (500) watts. For Asparagus Salad (top in picture), cut the cooked asparagus in 1¼ in. pieces. Mix a little salt with 1 lbs. lemon juice and ½ tsp. mustard. Stir in 4 tbs. oil, season with soy sauce and pepper. Mix this sauce with the lukewarm asparagus and sprinkle with chopped tarragon. The salad looks particularly attractive if both green and white asparagus are used.

Stuffed Mushrooms

Very easy, good value

85 calories per serving
Preparation time: 10 minutes
Cooking time: 2 (2¼) minutes

Serves: 2 people

6 large mushrooms
2 black olives
1 tbs. cream
1 tbs. brandy
Salt, pepper
1 tsp. butter

Trim and wash the mushrooms. Carefully remove the stalks and chop finely. Stone and chop the olives. Mix both with the cream and brandy. Season with salt and pepper. Fill the mushroom caps with the mixture. Place, rounded side down, in a dish greased with the butter. Cover and cook for 2 (2¼) minutes at 360 (330) watts.

Tip: The mushrooms can be sprinkled with freshly chopped marjoram or parsley before cooking. This adds more color to the dish.

Carrots with Orange

Very easy, good value

160 calories per serving
Preparation time: 10 minutes
Cooking time: 8 minutes

Serves: 2 people

1½ cups carrots
1 orange
Salt, pepper
½ tsp. sugar
1 tbs. butter

Peel and wash the carrots and thinly cut in ⅛ in. slices. Wash the orange in hot water, dry with paper towel and grate the rind, then squeeze the orange. Put the carrots in a dish with the orange juice and rind. Sprinkle with salt, pepper and sugar. Cut the butter in small pieces and add on top. Cover and cook for 8 minutes at 490 (500) watts.

Tip: Finely chopped chervil can be added to the carrots before serving.

Celery Root with Saffron Sauce

Very quick

130 calories per serving
Preparation time: 10 minutes
Cooking time: 7 (8) minutes

Serves: 2 people

1¼ cups celery root
Pinch saffron threads
1 tbs. butter
6 tbs. meat bouillon
Salt, pepper

Peel and wash the celery root and cut into sticks measuring ¼ in. by 1¼ in. Place the celery root in a dish. Add the saffron, butter, meat bouillon and a little salt and pepper. Cover and cook for 7 (8) minutes at 600 (500) watts, stirring the celery root 3 times during the cooking process.

Tip: Do not add too much saffron, so that the flavor of the celery root still comes through. Salt lightly, because the meat bouillon is already salted.

Leaf Spinach with Tomatoes

Very easy

140 calories per serving
Preparation time: 15 minutes
Cooking time: 4 (5) minutes

Serves: 2 people

1 onion
⅔ cup leaf spinach
1 tbs. butter
Salt, pepper, grated nutmeg
1 tsp. butter
5 cherry tomatoes
½ tsp. basil, freshly chopped

Peel and chop the onion. Wash the spinach thoroughly, drain and cut in strips. • Steam the butter and onion for 1 (1¼) minute at 600 (500) watts. Add the spinach, season with salt, pepper and nutmeg. Cover and cook for 2 (2½) minutes at 600 (500) watts. Butter a small shallow dish. Wash and halve the tomatoes and, with the rounded side underneath, place in the dish. Sprinkle with salt, pepper and basil and heat for 1 (1¼) minute at 360 (330) watts. • Arrange the spinach and place the tomatoes on top.

Tip: Tomato slices can be used instead of the cherry tomatoes.

Green Peas in Butter

Very quick

330 calories per serving
Preparation time: 10 minutes
Cooking time: 3 (3¾) minutes

Serves: 2 people

1 leek
3 tbs. butter
1 tbs. water
½ cup shelled peas
Salt, pepper

Trim and wash the leek and chop the white part. Put in a dish with 1 tbs. of the butter and water, cover and cook for 1 (1¼) minute at 600 (500) watts. • Add the peas, cover and cook for 2 (2½) minutes at 600 (500) watts. Cut the remaining butter in small pieces and mix into the peas. Season with salt and pepper.

Tip: If using frozen peas, add them frozen to the leek and increase the cooking time by 1 (1¼) minute.

Variations: For a change, at the beginning, add 2 oz. finely chopped ham. Or cook the peas with pearl onions and sprinkle with 1 tbs. freshly chopped mint.

Vegetable Curry

Very easy

120 calories per serving
Preparation time: 20 minutes
Cooking time: 11 (12) minutes

Serves: 2 people

⅓ cup cauliflower
⅓ cup green beans
⅓ cup celery root
⅓ cup carrots
1 small onion
3 tbs. white wine
1-2 tsp. curry powder
1 medium potato
3 tbs. meat bouillon
Salt, pepper
1 tsp. butter

Divide the cauliflower into small florets (remove the stalk and use in a soup). Halve the beans. Peel the celery root and the carrots. Wash and finely dice these vegetables. Peel and chop the onion. Put all the vegetables, except for the cauliflower and onion, in a dish with the white wine and curry powder, cover and cook for 5 (5½) minutes at 600 (500) watts. Peel, wash and finely dice the potato. Mix into the other vegetables with the cauliflower florets and onion and pour over the bouillon. Cover and cook for 6 (6½) minutes at 600 (500) watts. Season the vegetables with salt, pepper and finally a little curry powder. Mix the butter into the vegetables.

Tip: Rub 2 cups mango chutney through a sieve and mix into the vegetables. Or replace the bouillon with cream. Or leave out the potatoes and serve the dish mixed with a little cooked rice.

Vegetable Vol-Au-Vents

Delicious

550 calories per serving
Preparation time: 20 minutes
Cooking time: 10 (11¾) minutes

Serves: 2 people

½ cup mushrooms
⅔ cup asparagus
1 shallot
½ cup cauliflower or broccoli florets
1 tsp. chervil, freshly chopped
1 tbs. butter
Salt, pepper
3 tbs. meat bouillon
5 tbs. white wine
1 tsp. cornstarch
½ cup cream
2 vol-au-vent shells (bought ready-made)

Trim, wash and quarter the mushrooms. Peel and wash the asparagus and cut in small pieces, leaving the tips whole. Peel and finely chop the shallot. • Put the mushrooms in a dish with the asparagus, the washed cauliflower or broccoli, shallot, chervil and butter, and season with salt and pepper. Pour in the bouillon, cover and cook for 7 (8) minutes at 600 (500) watts. • Mix the white wine well with the cornstarch and cream. Stir into the vegetables and cook for 2 (2½) minutes at 600 (500) watts. • Heat the vol-au-vent shells for 1 (1½) minutes. Fill with the vegetable mixture and serve immediately.

Tip: The vegetable mixture can be changed according to seasonal availability.

Braised Lettuce

Very easy, good value

150 calories per serving
Preparation time: 10 minutes
Cooking time: 15 (16½) minutes
Serves: 2 people

4 heads of leaf or Boston lettuce
4¼ cups water
Salt, pepper, grated nutmeg
1 small onion
1 tbs. butter
½ cup meat bouillon

Trim and wash the lettuce and place in a shallow dish. Pour on the water and season with salt, pepper and nutmeg. Cover and cook for 2 (2½) minutes at 600 (500) watts. Peel and chop the onion. Take the lettuce out of the dish, drain well, remove the stalk and fold the leaves into flat bundles. Rinse out the dish, dry, butter and add the onion. Lay the bundles of lettuce in the dish. • Pour over the meat bouillon, cover and cook for 13 (14) minutes at 600 (500) watts.

Tip: Before cooking, you can wrap a thin bacon slice around each bundle. Chinese cabbage can also be used for the dish.

Variations: Fill the lettuce, before folding into bundles, with well seasoned ground beef, or serve it with a spicy tomatoe sauce. Alternatively, pour over a little cheese sauce and cook for an additional 5 minutes at 490 (500) watts.

Stuffed Leeks

Delicious

150 calories per serving
Preparation time: 15 minutes
Cooking time: 3 (3½) minutes
Serves: 4 people

2 leeks
2 oz. spicy sausage meat
1 egg yolk
3 tbs. cream
1 tbs. parsley, freshly chopped
Salt, pepper
1 tsp. butter
3 tbs. white wine

Trim and wash the leeks and remove any coarse green leaves. Cut in 4 in. long pieces. Cut the leek pieces in half lengthwise. Remove a little of the inside and chop very finely. Mix the chopped leek well with the sausage, egg yolk, cream and parsley. Season with salt and pepper. Pipe or spoon the mixture into the leeks. Butter a dish and place the stuffed leeks in it. Pour in the white wine and cook, covered, for 3 (3½) minutes at 600 (500) watts. Leave the leeks to stand, covered, for 5 minutes, so that they cook a little more.

Variations: Mashed potatoes and ground beef can be mixed with the chopped leeks and used to stuff the leeks. Cook as described above. Or mix ½ cup thick béchamel sauce (recipe page 38), with 1 tbs. grated cheese, the chopped leek and a little finely chopped ham, and fill the leeks.

Vichy Carrots

Very easy

85 calories per serving
Preparation time: 15 minutes
Cooking time: 8 (9) minutes

Serves: 4 people

1¾ cup young carrots
Salt
1 tsp. sugar
3 tbs. water
1 tbs. butter
1 tbs. parsley, freshly chopped

Trim and wash the carrots and cut in ¼ in. slices. Place in a suitable dish and sprinkle with salt and sugar. Add the water and the butter, cut in small pieces. Cover and cook for 8 (9) minutes at 600 (500) watts. Mix well and season to taste. Serve sprinkled with the parsley.

Variations: Madeira can be used instead of water. In this case add only ½ tsp. sugar. Small, whole, baby carrots can be prepared in the same way (leave on a little green top).

Buttered Corn on the Cob

Good value

260 calories per serving
Preparation time: 10 minutes
Cooking time: 9 (10) minutes

Serves: 2 people

2 corn on the cob
2 tbs. butter at room temperature
Salt, pepper

Remove the leaves and silk from the corn and wash. Mix the butter with a little salt and pepper and spread this on

the corn. • Heat a browning dish for 4 (4½) minutes at 600 (500) watts. Add the corn and cook uncovered for 5 (5½) minutes at 600 (500) watts. Serve immediately.

Tip: Corn on the cob prepared this way tastes excellent. If you prefer them steamed, they can be put in a dish with 2 tbs. water, covered, and cooked for 10 (11½) minutes at 600 (500) watts. In this case, serve the butter separately and pour over the hot corn at the table. Salted butter is preferable here.

Sugar Peas with Soy Sauce

More expensive

210 calories per serving
Preparation time: 20 minutes
Cooking time: 16 (16½) minutes

Serves: 2 people

1 onion
1 tsp. butter
1 cup sugar peas (snow peas)
1 tsp. soy sauce
¼ tsp. vinegar
3 tbs. water
Salt, pepper
1 tbs. butter

Peel and chop the onion and put in a dish with 1 tsp. butter. Cover and cook for 1 (1¼) minute at 600 (500) watts. String and wash the sugar peas and add to the dish. Mix the soy sauce, vinegar and water and pour over the vegetables. Sprinkle with a little salt and pepper. Cover and cook for 15 minutes at 490 (500) watts. Stir about every 3 minutes. Stir in the butter, cut in small pieces, before serving.

Red Cabbage in Wine

Very easy

150 calories per serving
Preparation time: 15 minutes
Cooking time: 41 (41½) minutes

Serves: 3 people

---
2 cups red cabbage
---
1 onion
---
1 tbs. butter

Pinch ground caraway
---
1 tsp. dill, freshly chopped

Salt, pepper

½ cup red wine

½ cup meat bouillon

Trim and halve the cabbage. Cut out the thick stems and the stalk. Wash the leaves and cut in fine strips. Peel and chop the onion and put in a dish with the butter. Cover and cook for 1 (1¼) minute at 600 (500) watts.

• Add the red cabbage, caraway and dill, a little salt and pepper, red wine and meat bouillon. Cover and cook for 40 (41½) minutes at 490 (500) watts.

Steamed Brussels Sprouts

Very quick

170 calories per serving
Preparation time: 15 minutes
Cooking time: 6 (6½) minutes

Serves: 2 people

1¼ cups Brussels sprouts
---
1 onion

Salt, pepper
---
3 tbs. water or meat bouillon
---
2 tbs. butter

Trim and wash the sprouts. Peel and chop the onion. Put the sprouts in a dish with the onion, a little salt and pepper,

water or bouillon, and cook, covered, for 6 (6½) minutes at 600 (500) watts. Drain the vegetables and add the butter, cut in small pieces.

Tip: Meat bouillon will give the sprouts a stronger flavor. The sprouts can be quartered, in which case reduce the cooking time to 2 minutes.

Steamed Salsify

Very easy

180 calories per serving
Preparation time: 15 minutes
Cooking time: 15 (17) minutes

Serves: 2 people

---
1 cup salsify
---
1 tbs. lemon juice
---
1 tbs. butter

½ cup meat or vegetable bouillon or water

Salt, pepper

Peel and wash the salsify, then cut in slices. Lay the salsify in water with lemon juice added, so that the vegetable does not discolor. Drain the salsify and put in a dish with the butter and bouillon or water. Season with salt and pepper. Cover and cook for 15 (17) minutes at 600 (500) watts. Drain and serve immediately.

Tip: Wear rubber gloves while peeling the salsify, otherwise your fingers will turn brown.

Braised Endive

Very easy

100 calories per serving
Preparation time: 10 minutes
Cooking time: 10 (11½) minutes

Serves: 4 people

4 head endive
Salt, pepper
3 tbs. meat bouillon or water
2 tbs. butter

Trim and wash the endive. Cut it in half lengthwise. Place the pieces side by side in a shallow dish. Season with salt and pepper and pour over the bouillon or water. Add the butter, cut in small pieces. Cover and cook for 10 (11½) minutes at 600 (500) watts. Leave covered for 2 minutes. Lift out of the juices and serve.

Tip: If you do not like the slightly bitter taste of endive, cut out a piece of the thick stalk before cooking. The juice which appears during the cooking can be poured off and reduced with 1 tbs. port or cream for 2 (2½) minutes, uncovered. Then pour the sauce over the vegetable.

Variations: Wrap the endive before cooking in 1 thin slice of bacon. Cook as described above. Alternatively, chop a hard-boiled egg and sprinkle over the endive with 2 tbs. chopped parsley. Heat 1 tbs. butter for 1 (1¼) minute and pour over.

Fennel with Mint

Delicious

260 calories per serving
Preparation time: 15 minutes
Cooking time: 9 (10½) minutes

Serves: 2 people

1⅔ cups fennel
Salt, pepper
1 tsp. mint, finely chopped
Pinch sugar
6 tbs. water
1 lime
2 tbs. butter
Pinch cayenne pepper

Trim and wash the fennel and cut in ¼ in. slices. Place in a dish and sprinkle with salt, pepper, mint and sugar. Pour over the water, cover and cook for 7 (8) minutes at 600 (500) watts. Wash the lime in hot water, dry and grate the peel. Squeeze the lime and add the juice and grated peel to the fennel. Mix well and cook covered, for an additional 2 (2½) minutes. Cut the butter into small pieces and mix in with the fennel before serving. Season to taste with cayenne pepper.

Tip: Sour cream can be added instead of butter. The lime juice can be replaced by freshly squeezed grapefruit or orange juice. In this case, use a little more cayenne pepper, leave out the mint or replace it with lemon balm.

Delicious Broccoli

Very easy, good value

240 calories per serving
Preparation time: 15 minutes
Cooking time: 8 (8¼) minutes

Serves: 2 people

1 cup broccoli
½ cup cream
1 tbs. water
Salt, pepper
½ tsp. root ginger, freshly grated, or ground ginger

Remove small florets of broccoli from the main stalk. Cut the stalks in ½ in. pieces. Wash the broccoli and place in a dish. Pour over about 6 tbs. of the cream and the water. Season with salt and pepper. Cover and cook for 7 minutes at 490 (500) watts. Take out of the dish. Add the remaining cream and the gin-

ger to the sauce. Cook for 1 (1¼) minute at 600 (500) watts. Pour the sauce over the broccoli.

Broccoli with Pine Kernels

An Italian speciality

170 calories per serving
Preparation time: 15 minutes
Cooking time: 8 (8¼) minutes

Serves: 2 people

1 cup broccoli
Salt, pepper
4 tbs. water
1 tbs. butter
1 tbs. pine kernels

Cut the florets off the stalks. Cut the stalks in ⅛ in. thick slices. Wash the broccoli. Put the broccoli pieces in a dish, place the florets on top and season with salt and pepper. Pour over

the water. Cover and cook for 7 minutes at 490 (500) watts. • Put the butter in a small dish with the pine kernels. Heat for 1 (1¼) minute at 600 (500) watts. Pour the water off the broccoli and add the pine kernels and butter to the dish.

Cauliflower with Ham and Parsley

Very easy

260 calories per serving
Preparation time: 15 minutes
Cooking time: 12 (12¾) minutes

Serves: 2 people

2 oz. cooked ham
1 tbs. butter
1¼ cups cauliflower florets
4 tbs. water
Salt, pepper
3 tbs. cream
2 tbs. parsley, freshly chopped

Finely dice the ham. Put in a dish with the butter and cook for 1 (1¼) minute at 600 (500) watts. Wash the cauliflower and add to the dish. Pour over the water and season with salt and pepper. Cover and cook for 9 minutes at 490 (500) watts. Add the cream and parsley and finish cooking for 2 (2½) minutes at 600 (500) watts.

Variation: Chop a hard-boiled egg, mix with 1 tbs. chopped parsley, 1 tbs. crumbs from a crispy roll and 1 tbs. butter. Heat for 1 (1¼) minute at 600 (500) watts. Top the cauliflower with this mixture.

Creamed Savoy Cabbage with Tarragon

Good value

480 calories per serving
Preparation time: 15 minutes
Cooking time: 16 (16½) minutes

Serves: 2 people

| 2 cups Savoy cabbage |
| 1 shallot |
| 1 tbs. butter |
| ½ tsp. flour |
| 2 tbs. white wine |
| ¾ cup cream |
| Salt, pepper |
| ½ tsp. tarragon, freshly chopped |

Trim and wash the cabbage. Remove the thick stems and cut the leaves in fine strips. Peel and chop the shallot and steam it in the butter for 2 (2½) minutes at 600 (500) watts. Add the cab-bage, mixing well, dust with the flour and pour over the wine and cream. Add a little salt, pepper and the tarragon and mix well. Cover and cook for 14 minutes at 490 (500) watts. Season to taste once more.

Tip: This dish will taste even bet-ter if the wine and cream are re-duced for 2 (2½) minutes at 600 (500) watts before adding the cabbage. In this case, do not use any flour.

Variation: 1⅔ cup trimmed leeks in ½ in. thick rings and steam with 1 tbs. butter for 2 (2½) minutes at 600 (500) watts. Cover and cook for an additional 8 minutes at 490 (500) watts.

Stuffed Swiss Chard

Very easy

85 calories per serving
Preparation time: 25 minutes
Cooking time: 9 (9¼) minutes

Serves: 4 people

| 4 cups Swiss chard |
| Salt, pepper |
| ½ cup vegetable bouillon |
| 2 tbs. butter |

Carefully remove the chard stalks, wash, drain and spread out the leaves on the work surface. Trim the stalks, wash and cut in ¾ in. strips. Lay these pieces on the leaves. Sprinkle with salt and pepper. Roll up the leaves and, with the ends underneath, lay in a wide dish. Pour the vegetable bouillon over the packages. Cover and cook for 8 minutes at 490 (500) watts. Take out the chard and drain well. • Put the butter in a small dish and melt for 1 (1¼) minute at 600 (500) watts. Sprinkle this over the chard.

Tip: You can use cream instead of vegetable bouillon, thickening the sauce after cooking with ½ tsp. cornstarch. The chard can also be prepared the same way as spinach, in which case they are chopped and steamed with shallots.

Variations: Fresh or frozen peas can be mixed in with the chard stalks. Or core a peeled tomato, cut in small pieces and wrap in the leaves with the stalks. Serve with a spicy tomato sauce.

Sauerkraut with Apple

Good value

170 calories per serving
Preparation time: 10 minutes
Cooking time: 51 (59¼) minutes

Serves: 3 people

1 onion	
1 tbs. butter	
1 apple	
2 cups sauerkraut	
1 bay leaf	
4-5 juniper berries	
1¾ cups meat bouillon	
½ cup white wine	
Pepper	

Peel and chop the onion and put in a dish with the butter. Cover and steam for 1 (1¼) minute at 600 (500) watts. Peel the apple and grate it, using the coarsest side of the grater. Add to the onion with the sauerkraut, bay leaf, the lightly crushed juniper berries, meat bouillon and white wine. Mix well, cover, and cook for 50 (58) minutes at 600 (500) watts, stirring every 10 minutes. Season with pepper. If there is too much juice when ready to serve, pour off a little.

Variations: In addition, add a finely grated potato to the cabbage. This will partially thicken the juices and the cabbage will have a milder flavor. Or steam a little diced bacon with the onion. Alternatively, add a little salt-pork to cook with the cabbage, in which case the cooking time should be lengthened according to the size and thickness of the pieces of meat.

Celery with Cider Sauce

Delicious

360 calories per serving
Preparation time: 10 minutes
Cooking time: 14 (15) minutes

Serves: 2 people

1 onion	
1 tbs. butter	
1⅔ cup celery	
1 tsp. flour	
Salt, pepper	
½ tsp. paprika powder	
3 tbs. cider	
4 tbs. milk	
½ cup cream	
½ tbs. parsley, freshly chopped	

Heat a browning dish for 2 (2½) minutes at 600 (500) watts. Peel and chop the onion and put in the dish with the butter. Steam for 2 (2½) minutes at 600 (500) watts. Trim and wash the celery and cut into ¾ in. long pieces. Mix with the onion. Cover and cook until soft for 1 minute at 490 (500) watts. Sprinkle with the flour, a little salt, pepper and the paprika. Pour over the cider, milk and cream. • Cover and cook for 5 minutes at 490 (500) watts. Remove the lid and cook for an additional 4 minutes at 490 (500) watts. Sprinkle with parsley.

Variations: Swiss chard can be prepared the same way. The cider can be replaced by white wine and the paprika omitted. Or peel and halve kohl rabi, cut it in ¼ in. slices and cook for 8 minutes at 490 (500) watts.

Stuffed Tomatoes with Spinach and Cottage Cheese

Very easy

290 calories per serving
Preparation time: 20 minutes
Cooking time: 3 minutes

Serves: 2 people

1 shallot
1 clove garlic
¼ cup leaf spinach
2 level tbs. walnuts, finely chopped
1 tsp. butter
2 tbs. creamed cottage cheese
1 egg yolk
1 tbs. Swiss cheese, freshly grated
Salt, pepper
2 large, firm tomatoes

Peel and finely chop the shallot. Peel and crush the

garlic. Pick over the spinach, wash thoroughly and chop coarsely. Put the shallot, garlic, spinach and walnuts in a buttered dish. Cook for 2 minutes at 490 (500) watts. Mix the cottage cheese with the egg yolk and cheese. Stir into the cooked mixture and season with salt and pepper. Wash the tomatoes and cut across in half. Hollow out a little and fill with the mixture. Place the tomatoes in the dish and cook, covered, for 1 minute at 490 (500) watts.

Tip: Cook, covered, 1 chopped shallot, ½ cup finely diced beets, 2 tbs. diced salami on cubes of toast, 1 tsp. chopped thyme and 1 tsp. butter, for 2 (2½) minutes 600 (500) watts. Season the mixture with salt and pepper and fill the prepared tomatoes. Cook for 1 minute at 490 (500) watts.

Onions Stuffed with Ground Meat

Delicious

210 calories per serving
Preparation time: 20 minutes
Cooking time: 12 (12½) minutes

Serves: 2 people

4 large onions
7 oz. ground meat
½ tsp. dried thyme
½ tsp. dried marjoram
2 tbs. stale white breadcrumbs
1 egg yolk
Salt, pepper
3 tbs. meat bouillon

Peel the onions. Cut off the top third of the onions and put aside. Hollow out the onions, taking care to leave 2 layers. Finely chop half of the onion centers (use the remainder for a soup or another dish). • Put the unseasoned ground meat in a

shallow dish and cook for 2 (2½) minutes at 600 (500) watts. Mix in the chopped onion, herbs, breadcrumbs and egg yolk. Season with salt and pepper and fill the onions with the mixture. Place the lids on top. Put the stuffed onions in a dish. Pour over the bouillon, cover, and cook for 10 minutes at 490 (500) watts.

Tip: This dish is particularly tasty when prepared with mild, purple onions.

Eggplant with Tomato

Easy to prepare and economical

260 calories per serving
Preparation time: 15 minutes
Cooking time: 5 (5½) minutes

Serves: 2 people

1½ tsp. butter
1 medium eggplant
2 large ripe tomatoes
Salt, pepper
2 tbs. ground hazelnuts
1 tsp. thyme leaves
1 clove garlic
1 tbs. freshly chopped parsley

Lightly butter a round, flat dish. Wash eggplant and tomatoes, remove hard core and cut in very thin slices. • Overlap alternating slices of the two vegetables in circles to fill dish. Sprinkle with salt, pepper, ground hazelnuts and thyme. Peel and crush garlic. Scatter with parsley and dabs of remaining butter over the vegetables. • Cover and cook for 5 (5½) minutes at 600 (500) watts.

Tip: This makes a good light accompaniment to risottos or meat served without sauce.

Variations: Replace eggplant with zucchini or potatoes cut in wafer-thin slices. Or alternatively, omit hazelnuts, thyme and parsley, instead sprinkling over plenty of basil and some extra garlic before serving. Or make the slices somewhat thicker and cook for 1 minute longer. Then cover dish with slices of any cheese that melts well and cook for an additional 1 minute at 490 (500) watts. Season well with pepper.

Peppers Stuffed with Sweetcorn

Easy to prepare and economical

220 calories per serving
Preparation time: 15 minutes
Cooking time: 7 (7½) minutes

Serves: 2 people

1 red or green pepper
Salt, pepper
1 onion
7 oz. canned sweetcorn
1 tbs. butter

Wash pepper, cut in half lengthwise, remove seeds and sprinkle with salt and pepper. Peel and chop onion, then divide between the two pepper halves. Fit halves together again in original shape and tie with kitchen thread. • Lay pepper in deep dish, cover and cook for 5 (5½) minutes at 600 (500) watts. • Remove thread, take out onion and lay separate halves back in dish. Mix together sweetcorn, butter cut in small pieces, onion and salt and pepper. • Fill pepper shells with mixture, cover and cook for 2 minutes 490 (500) watts.

Tip: To make the filling even more colorful, add some pieces of chopped red pepper and a few peas to the corn.

Ratatouille

Speciality from Nice

180 calories per serving
Preparation time: 15 minutes
Cooking time: 7½ (8¾) minutes
Serves: 4 people

1 medium eggplant
1 medium zucchini
3 tbs. olive
1 large onion
1 red pepper
2 ripe tomatoes
Salt, pepper
1 sprig each parsley, thyme and basil
1 bay leaf
3 cloves garlic
6 tbs. red wine

Wash eggplant and zucchini, remove stalks and cut in slices. Put olive oil into large dish and heat for ½ (¾) minute at 600 (500) watts. • Add eggplant slices to oil, cover and cook for 1 (1¼) minute at 600 (500) watts. • Peel and halve onion and cut in strips. Halve pepper, remove seeds, wash and cut in ¾ in. strips. Wash tomatoes, remove core, cut into 8 sections and gently squeeze out seeds and juice. Add prepared vegetables to eggplant, sprinkle lightly with salt and generously with pepper. Make a bouquet garni with parsley, thyme, basil and bay leaf. Peel garlic cloves and stir into vegetables with herbs. Pour on red wine. • Cover ratatouille and cook for 5 (5½) minutes at 600 (500) watts. Strain vegetables through a sieve and put juices back in dish. Reduce for 1 (1¼) minute at 600 (500) watts. • Remove bouquet garni and garlic from vegetables, season sauce according to taste and pour over vegetables.

Zucchini

Sophisticated, yet economical

170 calories per serving
Preparation time: 15 minutes
Cooking time: 7 (8) minutes

Serves: 4 people

1¼ cups zucchini	
2 tbs. water	
1 tsp. butter	
¼ cup Camembert	
2 eggs	
2 egg yolks	
3 tbs. cream	
Clove garlic	
Salt, pepper	
1 tsp. thyme leaves	

Wash zucchini, cut off stem and flower ends if necessary. Using a sharp knife or peeler, peel off a few very thin strips of skin lengthwise, then finely dice zucchini. • Put diced zucchini and water into a flat dish, laying strips of peel on top. Cover and cook for 3 (3½) minutes at 600 (500) watts. • Butter 4 small soufflé dishes (3 in. in diameter) and lay strips of peel in form of a cross in bottom of each. • Liquidize Camembert with eggs, egg yolks, cream and cooked zucchini. Peel garlic and crush before adding to the purée. Mix together garlic, salt, pepper and thyme. • Pour purée into dish and thicken for 2 (2¼) minutes at 180 (150) watts. • Spoon into prepared soufflé dishes. Cook one at a time for 2 (2¼) minutes at 180 (150) watts till set.

Tip: It is quicker to cook one serving at a time, since, when 2 are put in the microwave together, they require 6 minutes to set.

Sesame Zucchini

Simple to prepare, economical

75 calories per serving
Preparation time: 15 minutes
Cooking time: 4 minutes

Serves: 2 people

1 medium zucchini	
1 tsp. sesame oil	
1 clove garlic	
1 onion	
Salt, pepper	
1 tsp. sesame seeds	

Wash zucchini and dry with paper towel. Cut off stem and flower ends, then slice diagonally in pieces. Cut (½ in.) each individual slice at regular intervals from upper edge to lower, leaving skin intact at bottom. Flatten slightly to give a fan shape. • Brush a flat dish with sesame oil. Peel and halve garlic, then rub all over inside of dish. Peel and finely chop onion and scatter into dish. Sprinkle with salt and pepper and arrange zucchini "fans" neatly on top. Season again with salt and pepper. • Cover and cook for 3 minutes at 490 (500) watts. Remove lid, sprinkle zucchini with sesame seeds and cook for 1 more minute at 490 (500) watts.

Tip: For a spicier dish, sprinkle a small amount of soy sauce over zucchini. Remember that soy sauce is salty!

Leek and Potato Hotchpotch

Easy to prepare, economical

520 calories per serving
Preparation time: 20 minutes
Cooking time: 15 (17) minutes

Serves: 2 people

1⅔ cups leeks	
1¾ cups potatoes	
1 medium onion	
1 clove garlic	
3 tbs. white wine	
½ tsp. cornstarch	
6 tbs. cream	
6 tbs. milk	
1 tbs. butter	
Salt, pepper	

Clean and wash leeks, then cut in ½ in. rings. Peel and wash potatoes, before cutting in cubes. Peel and chop (¼ in. slices) onion. Peel and crush garlic. • Put leeks, potatoes, onion and garlic in a dish. Sprinkle with 2 tbs. of the white wine, cover and cook for 10 (11½) minutes at 600 (500) watts. • Mix cornstarch to a paste with cream and milk. Pour over vegetables and cook for 5 (5½) minutes at 600 (500) watts. • Stir butter and remaining white wine into vegetables and season to taste with salt and pepper.

Tip: Substituting cream for the milk makes this dish even more delicious, though richer too. However, the cornstarch can then be omitted.

Variation: Finely diced bacon may be added to the leek and potato.

Cheesy Potatoes

Easy to prepare, economical

310 calories per serving
Preparation time: 15 minutes
Cooking time: 15 (16) minutes

Serves: 4 people

2 cups potatoes	
1 tbs. butter	
Salt, pepper	
Ground nutmeg	
2 cloves garlic	
6 meat bouillon	
⅓ cup cream	
⅓ cup freshly grated Emmental cheese	
1 tbs. freshly chopped parsley	

Peel and wash potatoes, then cut in very thin slices. Butter a flat dish. • Layer potato slices in overlapping rows, seasoning with salt, pepper and nutmeg.

Peel and crush garlic, then sprinkle with potato. • Pour on meat bouillon and cream, cover and cook for 10 (10½) minutes at 360 (330) watts. • Scatter grated cheese over potato and cook uncovered for 5 (5½) minutes longer at 600 (500) watts. Sprinkle with parsley.

Tip: Cheese leftovers can be used in this recipe.

Variations: Thin slices of leek can be layered with the potato. Alternatively, the cheese may be omitted and thin slices of apple added to the potato. Or the potato may be covered with thin slices of bacon instead of cheese. Another possibility is to sprinkle caraway and paprika on the cheese. Or, a layer of precooked ground beef and chopped onion may be added to the potato.

Stuffed Potatoes

Economical

450 calories per serving
Preparation time: 20 minutes
Cooking time: 14 (16) minutes

Serves: 2 people

6 medium potatoes
6 tbs. salted water
1 tbs. sour cream
2 tbs. cream
1 egg yolk
4 tbs. freshly grated cheese
Pinch paprika
1 tbs. butter
1 tsp. freshly chopped basil
Salt, pepper

Peel and wash potatoes, put into dish with salted water, cover and cook for 12 (13½) minutes at 600 (500) watts. • Hollow out potatoes with sharp-edged spoon. Mash potato that has been removed, mixing well with sour cream, cream, egg yolk, cheese, paprika and butter. Stir in basil, seasoning to taste with salt and pepper. Fill potato shells with this mixture. • Arrange potatoes on plates and heat, covered, for 2 (2½) minutes at 600 (500) watts.

Variations: Cook 6 oz. poultry with 1 small chopped onion and 1 tsp. butter for 2 (2½) minutes at 600 (500) watts. Season to taste with salt, pepper and ½ tsp. chopped marjoram. Fill cooked, hollowed-out potatoes with meat and heat as above. Use remaining potato in some other way.

Potato and Apple Gratin

Easy to prepare

360 calories per serving
Preparation time: 20 minutes
Cooking time: 15½ (17¼) minutes

Serves: 2 people

2 large potatoes
1 apple
1 tbs. butter
1 tsp. flour
6 tbs. cream
6 tbs. milk
Salt, pepper
Ground nutmeg

Peel and wash potatoes, then using heavy-duty cutter, cut to fit size of ramekins (approx. 3 in). Slice trimmed potatoes ⅛ in. thick. Peel and core apple, then cut in equally thin slices. • Put half the butter in small dish and melt for ½ (¾) minute at 600 (500) watts. • Stir in flour. Then add cream and milk, and season with salt, pepper and nutmeg. • Cook sauce for 3 minutes at 490 (500) watts. Stir sauce twice during cooking time. • Grease 2 ramekins with remaining butter. • Mix potato slices with part of sauce, then layer in ramekins alternately with apple slices. Pour remaining sauce over layers. • Cover ramekins with plastic wrap and cook for 12 (13½) minutes at 600 (500) watts. Slightly loosen potato with knife around the outer edge and turn out onto plates.

Tip: If you have no cutting ring, you can use cookie cutters to shape potato rings individually.

Quick Lentil Dish

Easy to prepare

240 calories per serving
Preparation time: 25 minutes
Cooking time: 10 (11½) minutes

Serves: 4 people

½ cup brown lentils
⅔ cup potatoes
2-3 shallots
1 clove garlic
½ leek
1 small carrot
Piece celery root
¾ cup meat bouillon
Dash Tabasco
2 tbs. butter
Salt, pepper

C over lentils with lukewarm water and soak for 5 hours. • Peel potatoes and dice finely. Peel and chop shallots, peel and crush garlic. Clean and wash leek, carrot and celery root before cutting in fine julienne strips. • Drain lentils well and cook together with shallots, garlic and stock for 7 (8) minutes at 600 (500) watts in covered dish. • Blend one quarter of lentils with some cooking liquid in liquidizer. • Mix remaining lentils with vegetables and Tabasco, cover and cook for 3 (3½) minutes at 600 (500) watts. • Add lentil purée, butter and season to taste with salt and pepper.

Tricolor Lentils

Excellent, economical

380 calories per serving
Preparation time: 20 minutes
Cooking time: 10 (11½) minutes

Serves: 2 people

¼ cup brown, green and red lentils
1 onion
1 clove garlic
1 tbs. butter
1 bay leaf
1¼ cups meat bouillon
Salt, pepper
1 tsp. butter

S oak three kinds of lentils separately in cold water overnight. • Peel and chop onion and peel and crush garlic. Chop onion and crush garlic. Mix both with drained brown lentils, ¾ cups butter, bay leaf and bouillon in a dish, cover and cook for 3 (3½) minutes at 600 (500) watts. • Add drained green lentils and cook for another 3 (3½) minutes at 600 (500) watts. • Add drained red lentils together with remaining bouillon and cook for 4 (4½) minutes at 600 (500) watts. • Season to taste with salt and pepper and stir in butter in small pieces.

Tip: The cooking time for lentils can vary greatly, depending not only on the variety, but also on length of storage. Since this can never be known exactly, lentils should be tested after each cooking period and cooked longer if necessary.

Chili Con Carne

Easy to prepare

670 calories per serving
Preparation time: 30 minutes
Cooking time: 72 (72½) minutes

Serves: 2 people

7 tbs. borlotti or white beans	
1 large onion	
2 cloves garlic	
1 cup peeled tomatoes (canned)	
1 tbs. olive oil or butter	
7 oz. beef, chuck	
1 medium carrot	
Piece celery root	
1 small green pepper	
¾ cup red wine	
1 cup meat bouillon	
Sprig fresh thyme	
1 bay leaf	
1 tbs. tomato purée	
1 tsp. chili paste or powder	

Cover beans with cold water and leave to soak overnight. • Peel and finely chop onion and garlic. Drain and chop tomatoes, put in dish with onion, garlic and oil or butter. • Cook for 2 (2½) minutes at 600 (500) watts. • Cut meat in very small cubes. Clean, wash and finely dice carrot, celery root and pepper. Add prepared vegetables, meat, red wine, bouillon, drained beans, thyme, bay leaf, tomato purée and half of the chili to onion mixture. • Mix thoroughly, cover and cook for 70 minutes at 490 (500) watts. During cooking time, stir every 20 minutes and check that there is enough liquid in dish. Add more bouillon if necessary. • Season to taste with salt, pepper and remaining chili paste or powder before serving.

Tip: The flavor of this dish is improved by leaving it to stand, still covered, for a few minutes once the actual cooking time is over. Canned beans can also be used, in which case the cooking time is about 30 minutes shorter, and only ⅓ cup each of red wine and bouillon are required.

Black Bean with Beansprouts

Easy to prepare, economical

230 calories per serving
Soaking time: overnight
Preparation time: 5 minutes
Cooking time: 43 (43½) minutes

Serves: 2 people

¼ cup black beans	
1 tbs. butter	
2½ cups water	
Salt	
⅔ cup beansprouts	
½ tsp. soy sauce	
1 tbs. sherry	
½ tsp. sesame oil	
Pepper	
8 leaves radicchio	

Cover black beans with cold water and soak overnight • Drain beans, add butter, water and pinch salt, then cook for 40 minutes at 490 (500) watts. • Cook beansprouts, soy sauce, sherry and sesame oil, covered, for 3 (3½) minutes, at 600 (500) watts. Season with salt and pepper. • Wash and drain radicchio leaves before arranging on serving dish. Mix beans with beansprouts and arrange on top.

Desserts and Drinks

Microwave ovens are also absolutely ideal for preparing delicious desserts, particularly those which, prepared in the traditional way, require a lot of time and a dash of luck to be completely successful. A good example is Chocolate Mousse, produced without any difficulty and in a very few minutes in your microwave. Even such time-consuming procedures as cooking in a double boiler are superfluous with a microwave. Custards and blancmanges are amazingly quick and simple to make.

And for the odd occasion when visitors arrive unexpectedly in the afternoon, the ingredients for an almond cake or a jelly roll can be quickly combined and "baked" in your microwave.

If you occasionally feel you would like a hot drink, you need only stir together the ingredients in a heat-resistant glass and within a matter of minutes your hot chocolate, mulled wine or tea is ready.

Apricot Jellies

Easy to prepare

220 calories per serving
Preparation time: 15 minutes
Cooking time: 12 (13½) minutes

Serves: 4 people

| 2 cups apricots |
| ⅔ cup sugar |
| ½ cup water |
| 3 tbs. white wine |
| 2 tbs. cornstarch |
| 1 tbs. apricot brandy |

Wash and dry apricots, then halve them and remove pits. Put halves into a deep dish. • Add sugar, water and white wine, cook for 5 (5½) minutes at 600 (500) watts. • Take out half the apricots (preferably those which are still firm), and cut in slices. Cook remaining apricots for 5 (5½) minutes longer at 600 (500) watts, before rubbing through a fine sieve. • Mix together purée, cornstarch and apricot brandy. Cook for 2 (2½) minutes at 600 (500) watts. • Stir in apricot slices. • Spoon into pretty glasses and place in refrigerator for several hours. • Serve decorated with whipped cream.

Tip: This dessert can also be prepared with rhubarb, plums or citrus fruits. With rhubarb you must add more sugar and a little lemon juice, omitting the apricot brandy. With plums, plum brandy is appropriate, whereas with citrus fruits, either gin or orange liqueur would be suitable.

Pears in Red Wine

Rather more expensive

400 calories per serving
Preparation time: 10 minutes
Cooking time: 13 (14½) minutes

Serves: 2 people

| 4 tbs. sugar |
| 2 tbs. water |
| ¾ cup good dry red wine |
| 3 tbs. cassis liqueur |
| ½ stick cinnamon |
| 1 clove |
| 4 firm pears |

Caramelize sugar and water for 4 (4½) minutes at 600 (500) watts. • Add wine, liqueur, cinnamon stick and clove. Cook for 4 (4½) minutes at 600 (500) watts. • Peel pears, removing base but leaving stalk. • Place pears in red wine syrup, cover and cook for 5 (5½) minutes at 600 (500) watts. • Serve pears either still warm or well chilled.

Tip: Try to choose a deep, narrow dish to cook pears so that they are completely covered by the liquid. This will ensure an even red color.

Variations: Apples can be prepared in the same way. However, the cooking time will be somewhat longer, according to variety. The cooked apples should be tender without collapsing altogether. • Both pears and apples in red wine may be garnished with chopped pistachio nuts. Or they may be served on vanilla or nut ice cream, coated with the warm wine syrup. Or else they may be served sprinkled with toasted flaked almonds on a base of whipped cream, with the syrup served separately.

Grandmother's Apple Compote

Easy to prepare

500 calories per serving
Preparation time: 15 minutes
Cooking time: 12 (13½) minutes

Serves: 2 people

1¼ cups apple juice
1 tbs. raisins
2 large apples (firm variety)
¼ cup butter
1 tbs. sugar
Pinch cinnamon

Cook apple juice, covered, for 2 (2½) minutes at 600 (500) watts. Wash raisins and soak in the hot juice. • Peel and core apples, then cut in slices. • Pour juice off raisins and mix them in a dish with the apple slices, half of the butter, the sugar and the cinnamon. Cover and cook for 6 (6½) minutes at

360 (330) watts. Turn several times during cooking so that apples are evenly done. • Serve compote warm.

French Cherry Pudding

French specialty

480 calories per serving
Preparation time: 20 minutes
Cooking time: 8 minutes

Serves: 2 people

1 tbs. butter
2 eggs
¼ cup sugar
1 vanilla pod
⅓ cup milk
Pinch salt
1 tbs. rum
⅓ cup flour
1¼ cups black cherries
Powdered sugar

Grease flan dish with butter. • Whisk eggs with sugar till fluffy. Slit vanilla pod lengthwise, scrape out inside and mix into egg, together with milk, salt and rum. Sieve flour and stir in. • Put half mixture into dish. Wash and stone cherries, spread on top and cover with rest of mixture. • Cook for 8 minutes at 490 (500) watts. Serve warm dusted with powdered sugar.

Aromatic Prunes

Extremely quick

310 calories per serving
Preparation time: 15 minutes
Cooking time: 8 (4½) minutes

Serves: 3 people

¾ cup water
1 tbs. tea leaves
3 tbs. sugar
1 cup stoned prunes

1 tbs. red wine
2 tsp. cornstarch

Heat water in covered dish for 3 (3½) minutes at 600 (500) watts. • Pour over tea leaves and let stand for 3 minutes. Strain and combine tea with sugar and prunes. Cook for 3 (3½) minutes at 600 (500) watts. Strain. Mix liquid with red wine and cornstarch, cook for 2 (2½) minutes at 600 (500) watts. • Pour syrup over prunes and serve either warm or cold.

Pears with Ginger

Easy to prepare

310 calories per serving
Preparation time: 15 minutes
Cooking time: 10 (11½) minutes

Serves: 4 people

4 pears (firm variety)
4 pieces candied ginger
¾ cup white wine
1 cup sugar
4 tbs. cranberry sauce

Peel pears, cut in half lengthwise and remove core. Cut a little off rounded side so that pear sits firmly and lay halves, cut side down, in a suitable dish. Finely chop ginger, and sprinkle over pears with sugar. Pour wine over. • Cover and cook pears for 10 (11½) minutes at 600 (500) watts. • Fill with cranberry sauce while still warm.

Tip: Excellent not only as a dessert but also to accompany game dishes.

Apricot Compote

Economical

240 calories per serving
Preparation time: 5 minutes
Cooking time: 4 (4½) minutes

Serves: 4 people

1 cup dried apricots
¼ cup sugar
2 tbs. apricot brandy (optional)

Cover dried apricots with cold water, cover and soak overnight. • Next day, put apricots, with soaking water, and sugar in a dish. • Cover and cook 4 (4½) minutes at 600 (500) watts. Add brandy if desired.

Tip: Prunes can also be prepared in this way, with the addition of plum brandy to provide the aroma.

Tipsy Figs

More expensive

210 calories per serving
Preparation time: 15 minutes
Cooking time: 12 (13½) minutes

Serves: 4 people

6 tbs. white wine
1 cup sugar
1 stick cinnamon
2–3 cloves
6 tbs. orange juice
3 tbs. lemon juice
8 large fresh purple figs

Put wine, sugar, crushed cinnamon stick, cloves and orange and lemon juice into a dish. Cover and cook for 4 (4½) minutes at 600 (500) watts. • Remove lid, take out cinnamon and cloves and reduce sauce by cooking for another 8 (9) minutes at 600 (500) watts. • Wash figs, drain and pat dry on kitchen towel. Add to hot sauce for 2 minutes, so that they are just warmed through. Serve figs on plates with sauce poured round them.

Three-Fruit Compote

Easy to prepare

210 calories per serving
Preparation time: 15 minutes
Cooking time: 13 (14) minutes

Serves: 4 people

2 pears (firm variety)
2 apples
Rind of ½ lemon
1 stick cinnamon
3 tbs. sugar
1⅔ cups plums

Peel pears and apples, cut each in eighths and remove core. Put into suitable dish and add 2–3 tbs. water. • Cover and cook fruit for 5 (5½) minutes at 600 (500) watts. Cut lemon peel in very fine strips and add to fruit with cinnamon and sugar. • Wash, halve and stone plums before combining with other fruit. • Cover and continue to cook for

8 (8½) minutes at 360 (330) watts. Add 1–2 tbs. water halfway through if too little juice has formed.

Tip: In winter, fresh plums can be replaced by soaked prunes.

Rhubarb Compôte

Extremely quick

400 calories per serving
Preparation time: 10 minutes
Cooking time: 5 minutes

Serves: 2 people

2 cups rhubarb
⅓ cup white wine
⅔ cup sugar
½ stick cinnamon

Peel and wash rhubarb, then cut in 1½ in. pieces. Combine pieces with white wine, sugar and cinnamon stick in a

suitable dish. • Cover and cook for 5 minutes at 490 (500) watts. • Allow compôte to cool and remove cinnamon stick.

Caramelized Pears

Economical

210 calories per serving
Preparation time: 10 minutes
Cooking time: 5 (5¾) minutes

Serves: 2 people

2 large pears
2 tbs. sugar
½ tbs. butter
3 tbs. apple juice

Wash pears and cut in eight pieces, leaving peel on. Remove core, then put segments in dish with sugar and butter. • Caramelize pears for 4 (4½) minutes at 600 (500) watts until they change color. • Pour on ap-

ple juice, cover and cook pears another 1 (1¾) minutes at 600 (500) watts.

Tip: The pears change color more quickly in a browning dish and also taste more strongly of caramel. • Red apples can be treated equally well in this way. Or plums can be halved and briefly caramelized, with red wine added instead of apple juice and only 3 (3½) minutes for caramelizing and ½ (¾) minute for final cooking.

Semolina and Raspberry Pudding

Easy to prepare

290 calories per serving
Preparation time: 10 minutes
Cooking time: 17 (17½) minutes

Serves: 4 people

2 cups milk
2 tbs. sugar
Pinch salt
1 tsp. grated lemon rind
1 tsp. lemon juice
1½ tbs. butter
¼ cup semolina
1 egg, separated
1 cup frozen raspberries

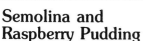

Put milk in dish with sugar, salt, lemon rind, lemon juice and 3 tbs. of the butter. Cover and cook for 6 (6½) minutes at 600 (500) watts. • Add semolina and beaten egg yolk, mixing together well. Cover and cook for another 7 minutes at 490 (500) watts. • Beat egg white until stiff and fold into mixture once it has cooled slightly. • Grease 4 jello molds with remaining butter. Fill with semolina and place in refrigerator. Turn out on plates once set. • Before serving, defrost raspberries in microwave for 4 minutes on defrost control. Liquidize ¾ cup of the raspberries and rub through a fine sieve. Pour sauce round semolina shapes and decorate with remaining whole raspberries.

Variations: More simply, slightly diluted raspberry syrup may be poured over the semolina shapes. Other berries may be used instead of raspberries. As an alternative sauce, passion fruit purée tastes delicious.

Fluffy Wine Cream

Extra quick to prepare

310 calories per serving
Preparation time: 10 minutes
Cooking time: 5 minutes

Serves: 4 people

6 tbs. sugar
¾ cup white wine
Juice of ½ lemon
½ grated lemon rind
3 eggs
1 cup whipping cream

Whisk sugar with white wine, lemon juice, lemon rind and eggs until light and foamy. • Put into dish, cover and cook for 5 minutes at 490 (500) watts. • Whisk for 2 minutes with balloon whisk or electric beater, then chill briefly. • Whip cream until stiff and fold into cooled wine cream. • Put into chilled glasses and leave in refrigerator until ready to serve.

Tip: Cover wine cream with kitchen foil while cooling to avoid contamination by other foodstuffs.

Variations: Skinned and seeded grapes may be stirred into the cream. Or ice cream may be put into the glasses, with chopped fruit or berries as the next layer and the wine cream poured on top. Finally, the sweet can be browned quickly under a hot grill.

Caramel Cream

Sophisticated

330 calories per serving
Preparation time: 30 minutes
Cooking time: 9 (10) minutes

Serves: 4 people

| ½ vanilla pod |
| 1 cup cream |
| Pinch cinnamon |
| ⅓ cup sugar |
| 3 egg yolks |
| 2 dashes lemon juice |
| ¼ cup whipped cream |

Slit vanilla pod lengthwise, put in dish with cream and cinnamon and heat for 3 (3½) minutes at 600 (500) watts. • Whisk ¼ cup of the sugar with egg yolks until they form a thick white cream. Stir this egg mixture into the hot cream and warm for 3 minutes at 490 (500) watts. • Beat mixture lightly 2–3 times with balloon whisk during cooking. • Remove from microwave as soon as mixture has thickened. • Put remaining sugar into browning dish and add 1 tbs. with lemon juice. Heat for 3 (3½) minutes at 600 (500) watts until sugar is golden brown. • This stage must be watched very carefully to avoid burning sugar. Remove sugar from oven as soon as it is caramelized. • Pour warm cream mixture onto caramel and stir until dissolved. Cool, stirring occasionally. Remove vanilla pod. • Spoon into bowls or glasses and garnish with rosettes of whipped cream.

Chocolate Mousse

Specialty from France

520 calories per serving
Preparation time: 10 minutes
Cooking time: 3 minutes
Chilling time: several hours

Serves: 4 people

| 6 oz. plain chocolate |
| ⅓ cup cream |
| 2 egg yolks |
| 1 egg white |
| 1 tbs. sugar |
| ¾ cup whipped cream |

Break chocolate into pieces, put in dish with unbeaten cream, cover and heat for 3 minutes at 490 (500) watts. • Whisk egg yolks and stir into chocolate. Beat egg white until stiff and fold in the sugar. This mixture is in turn, folded into the slightly cooled chocolate mixture. Fold in whipped cream. Put into refrigerator for several hours to set.

Tip: If the mousse is left to set in a bowl, it may be served in egg-shaped mounds formed by using a spoon dipped in hot water. However, it is easier to put the mousse into pretty dessert glasses before placing in the refrigerator.

Stuffed Burgundy Apples

Easy to prepare

330 calories per serving
Preparation time: 15 minutes
Cooking time: 6 (6½) minutes

Serves: 4 people

4 firm apples
1¼ cups red burgundy
1 cup sugar
½ stick cinnamon
2 cloves
For the filling:
1 cup full-cream curd cheese
2 tbs. sugar
½ tsp. grated lemon rind
1 tsp. chopped pistachios

Peel apples, cut in half, across, and remove core. Lay apples in dish with cut surface down. Combine wine with sugar and pour over apples. Add cinnamon and cloves. • Cover and cook apples for 6 (6½) minutes at 600 (500) watts. • Allow to cool. Combine cheese with sugar and lemon rind, fill hollows in cooled upturned apples and sprinkle with pistachios.

Tip: Turn apples halfway through cooking time so that they are evenly colored.

Stuffed Apples with Vanilla Sauce

Economical

480 calories per serving
Preparation time: 15 minutes
Cooking time: 10 minutes

Serves: 2 people

2 large firm apples (e.g. Golden Delicious)
3 tbs. raisins
2 tbs. orange liqueur
1 tsp. sugar
1 tbs. sour cream
For the sauce:
¾ cup milk
2 tbs. vanilla pudding
1 tbs. sugar

Wash and core apples, taking care not to break through the skin on the underside. Wash and drain raisins, then combine with orange liqueur, sugar and sour cream. Allow to stand for 30 minutes. • Put apples in dish, fill with raisin mixture, cover and cook for 7 minutes at 490 (500) watts. • Arrange apples on plates and pour cooking juice over them. • Mix together milk, vanilla pudding and sugar for sauce. Cook for 3 minutes at 490 (500) watts. Stir well and serve separately with apples.

Tip: It is essential to choose a firm cooking variety of apple to avoid ending up with apple sauce (i.e. do not use Bramleys).

Variations: Fill apples with mixture of 1 tbs. raspberry jam and 2 tbs. ground hazelnuts or almonds. Or the vanilla sauce may be replaced by a sauce made with berries, e.g. blackberries. Cook 1 cup blackberries with 2 tbs. preserving sugar and 3 tbs. water for 2 (2½) minutes at 600 (500) watts. Rub through a sieve and serve warm with apples.

Rotegrüze a Tamons German Dessert

Rather more expensive

180 calories per serving
Preparation time: 20 minutes
Cooking time: 15 (15¾) minutes
Chilling time: several hours

Serves: 6 people

1 cup raspberries
1 cup strawberries
¾ cup blackberries
¾ cup bilberries
¾ cup stoned black cherries
¾ cup sugar
6 tbs. water

Wash and drain fruit, mix with sugar and allow to stand for 5–10 minutes. Mix cornstarch with water. • Put fruit and cornstarch mixture into a suitable dish, cover and cook for 15 (15¾) minutes at 360 (330) watts. • Rub two-thirds of the fruit through a fine sieve; halve or quarter remaining fruit if necessary, then add to purée. • Put into pretty serving bowls and place in refrigerator for a few hours to set. • Serve according to taste with chilled pouring cream.

Variations: Frozen fruit may be used for this recipe. It should first be thawed for 5 (5½) minutes in a covered dish at 600 (500) watts. Since frozen berry fruit is sometimes slightly sweetened, the amount of sugar should be reduced accordingly. A really excellent version can be made with rhubarb and strawberries; chop rhubarb in ½ in. pieces and cook with sliced strawberries as above. Use juice from rhubarb instead of water to mix with cornstarch.

Pears with Chocolate Delight

Sophisticated

230 calories per serving
Preparation time: 15 minutes
Cooking time: 5½ (6¾) minutes

Serves: 4 people

2 large pears (firm variety)
1½ tbs. sugar
3 oz. plain chocolate
3 tbs. cream
1 tbs. brandy
1 egg white
Pinch salt
4 mint leaves

Peel, halve and core pears. Cut through rounded side of pear halves and lay in dish, flat side down. • Cover and cook pears for 2½ (3) minutes at 600 (500) watts. Sprinkle with 1 tbs. of the sugar, cover and cook again for 1 (1¾) minutes at 600 (500) watts. • Break chocolate in pieces and put in a dish with the cream. Melt for 2 (2½) minutes at 600 (500) watts. Mix thoroughly with a whisk and add brandy. Beat egg white with remaining sugar and salt until soft peaks form, then fold into chocolate. • Arrange each pear half on plate, rounded side up. Pour chocolate either over or beside pear, garnishing with a mint leaf.

Filled Pancakes

Sophisticated

290 calories per serving
Standing time: 1 hour
Preparation time: 25 minutes
Cooking time: 7 minutes

Serves: 4 people

¼ cup flour
6 tbs. milk
1 egg
Pinch salt
2 tbs. sugar
2 tbs. butter
For the filling:
1 cup strawberries
2 tbs. strawberry jam
3 tbs. cream
1 tbs. sugar
For the sauce:
¾ cup strawberries
1 tbs. sugar
1 tbs. water

Mix flour with milk, salt and sugar, stirring well. Allow batter to stand for 1 hour. • Wash strawberries for filling, then hull and chop them before mixing with jam. Beat cream with sugar until stiff and put in refrigerator. • Wash and hull strawberries for sauce, then liquidize with sugar and water. • Lightly butter shallow round Pyrex dish 6 in. diameter and pour in a thin layer of batter. • Cook for 1 minute at 490 (500) watts. Turn out onto aluminum foil and keep warm. • Cook 3 more crêpes in the same way and keep warm. • Put strawberry purée into a small dish and heat for 3 minutes at 490 (500) watts. • Fold whipped cream into strawberry filling. Fill crêpes with mixture and roll up.

Fluffy Raisin Omelette

Economical

290 calories per serving
Preparation time: 20 minutes
Cooking time: 6 (6¾) minutes

Serves: 2 people

2 tbs. raisins
2 tbs. rum
2 egg yolks
1 tsp. vanilla sugar
3 egg whites
Pinch salt
1 tbs. sugar
1 tbs. whipped cream
1 tsp. butter
Powdered sugar

Wash and drain raisins, mix in dish with rum and allow to stand until raisins have absorbed all the liquid. • Whisk egg yolks with vanilla sugar until fluffy. Beat egg whites with salt and sugar until stiff. Mix raisins into yolk cream, then fold in beaten egg white and whipped cream. • Grease a large flat dish with the butter and heat for 1 (1¼) minute at 600 (500) watts. • Put egg mixture into dish and cook for 3 (3¼) minutes at 360 (300) watts. Remove dish from microwave and loosen omelette around the edge with spatula. Cook for another 2 (2¼) minutes at 360 (330) watts, fold over in half and serve at once, dusted with powdered sugar.

Tip: A filling may also be added to this omelette. Leave out raisins and add filling after first cooking period, finishing the process as described above.

Chocolate Almond Cake

Sophisticated

2600 calories per serving
Preparation time: 20 minutes
Cooking time: 11 (12) minutes

Serves: 1½ quart cake dish

5 eggs, separated
1 cup sugar
Pinch salt
1¾ cups ground almonds
3½ oz. plain chocolate
10 blanched almonds

Whisk egg yolks with half the sugar and salt to a fluffy white cream. Beat egg whites with remaining sugar till stiff. Mix ground almonds into yolk cream, then fold egg white in carefully. Line cake dish with waxed paper and spoon mixture in. • Bake cake for 5 (5¼) minutes at 360 (330) watts, then for an additional 5 (5½) minutes at 600 (500) watts. • Take cake out of microwave, allow to cool for 5-10 minutes before turning out onto a cooling rack and leave until completely cool. Place rack over a piece of aluminum foil. • Break chocolate in pieces, put into a small dish and melt at 600 (500) watts for 1 (1¼) minute. Spread chocolate evenly over cake and garnish with blanched almonds.

Variations: Alternatively, the cake may be garnished with candied fruit. A richer cake results from the addition of a large, finely grated carrot with ½ tsp. grated lemon rind to the basic mix.

Poor Knights

Easy to prepare, economical

520 calories per serving
Preparation time: 15 minutes
Cooking time: 5 minutes, 10 seconds

Serves: 2 people

2 eggs
2 tbs. milk
1 tbs. cream
Pinch of salt
1 tsp. grated lemon rind
4 thin slices white bread without crusts
1 tbs. thick plum jam
2 tbs. clarified butter
½ tsp. cinnamon
2 tbs. sugar

Beat eggs slightly and mix thoroughly with milk and cream, adding salt and lemon rind. • Spread plum jam on one side of bread and put 2 slices together, spread sides facing. • Heat browning dish for 4 (4½) minutes at 600 (500) watts. • Dip bread into egg mixture. Put clarified butter into dish and press bread onto this. Brown for 20 seconds at 490 (500) watts on each side. • Pour remaining egg mixture over bread and cook for another ½ minute at 490 (500) watts. • Combine sugar and cinnamon, sprinkling over the bread sandwiches before serving warm.

Variations: Apricot jam or marmalade can be used instead of plum jam.

Mocha Cream

Easy to prepare

310 calories per serving
Preparation time: 15 minutes
Cooling time: 15 minutes

Serves: 4 people

2 tbs. instant coffee powder

3 tbs. sugar

4 egg yolks

¾ cup whipping cream

1 egg white

Whisk together coffee powder, 2 tbs. of the sugar, egg yolks and 2 tbs. of the cream until light and fluffy. • Put into a dish and cook for 3 (3¼) minutes at 360 (330) watts, stirring every 30 seconds. • Stir mixture until completely cooled. Whisk rest of cream until stiff and fold three quarters of it into mixture. Whisk egg white with the remaining sugar until stiff and fold into mixture. • Put into

pretty glasses and decorate with remaining whipped cream.

Variations: Instant chocolate may be used instead of coffee, though less sugar will be needed if it is sweetened.

Praline Orange Cream with Chocolate Sauce

Sophisticated

570 calories per serving
Preparation time: 30 minutes
Cooking time: 7 (8¼) minutes

Serves: 4 people

½ cup sugar

2 tbs. water

2½ tbs. blanched, ground almonds

1 tsp. butter

1 orange

3 egg yolks

¾ cup milk

4 tsp. gelatine

1 tbs. orange liqueur

¾ cup whipping cream

For the sauce:

2 oz. plain chocolate

1½ tbs. cream

Put about ⅓ cup of the sugar with water into a dish and allow to caramelize for 2¾ (3¼) minutes at 600 (500) watts. • Add ground almonds and mix in well. Butter a large piece of aluminum foil and spread mixture onto it. • When it has cooled, crush finely with a rolling pin. • Wash orange in hot water, grate rind and squeeze juice. • Whisk together egg yolks, remaining sugar, orange rind and juice until fluffy. • Heat milk for 2 (2½) minutes at 600 (500) watts. Add to the yolk mixture, stirring well. Cook for 2 minutes at 490 (500)

watts to a thickened cream. • Soak gelatine in cold water. Add to warm cream with orange liqueur and stir till dissolved. • Mix crushed praline into cooled orange cream. Beat cream till stiff and fold into the yolk mixture. Spoon into dessert bowls or individual molds and leave to set in refrigerator. • For the sauce, break chocolate into pieces and put in a dish with the cream. Heat for ¼ (½) minute at 600 (500) watts. • Before serving, dip bowls or molds quickly into hot water and turn orange creams out onto plates. Pour chocolate sauce around base.

Semolina Flummery with Raspberry Sauce

Sophisticated

450 calories per serving
Preparation time: 20 minutes
Cooking time: 17 (18) minutes

Serves: 4 people

2 cups milk	
4 tbs. sugar	
Pinch salt	
3 tbs. butter	
1 vanilla pod	
6 tbs. semolina	
2 egg yolks	
⅓ cup cream	
1 cup raspberries	
For the sauce:	
¾ cup raspberries	
¼ cup sugar	
6 tbs. water	
Juice of 1 lemon	

Combine milk, sugar, salt and butter in a dish. Slit vanilla pod lengthwise and scrape out into milk mixture. • Heat for 6 (6½) minutes at 600 (500) watts. • Stir in semolina, then cook at 360 (330) watts for 11 (11½) minutes, stirring occasionally. • Cool briefly before mixing in egg yolks. Whip cream until stiff and fold into cooled mixture. Rinse out mold with cold water and fill with mixture. Chill until flummery is set. • To make the sauce, liquidize washed raspberries with sugar, water and lemon juice, then rub through a sieve to remove seeds. • Turn flummery out onto a serving dish, pour sauce around it and decorate with whole raspberries.

Cremes Brulees

Easy to prepare

480 calories per serving
Preparation time: 20 minutes
Cooking time: 10½ (11½) minutes

Serves: 4 people

¼ cup sugar	
1 tbs. water	
2 egg yolks	
1 egg	
Pinch salt	
¼ cup sugar	
1 vanilla pod	
1 cup whipping cream	
1 tbs. rum	
1 tsp. sugar	

Put 1 tbs. of the sugar and 1 tsp. of the water in each of 4 individual soufflé dishes (3 in.) and caramelize at 600 (500) watts for 3½ (4) minutes. If sugar browns unevenly, turn dishes during cooking process. • Whisk egg yolks and egg with salt and sugar until fluffy. Slit vanilla pod lengthwise and scrape inside into egg mixture, stirring in with ¾ cup of the cream and the rum. Divide between soufflé dishes and cover with plastic wrap. • Cook for 7 (7½) minutes at 180 (150) watts until firm, then chill for several hours. • Whip remaining cream till stiff. Run a knife round top of dishes to loosen creams before turning out onto plates and decorating with whipped cream.

Tip: A Caramel Sauce can be made in the following way and served separately with the creams: caramelize ⅓ cup sugar with 2 tbs. water for 4 (4½) minutes at 600 (500) watts. Add ¼ cup water and 2 tbs. butter and cook for an additional 2 minutes at 490 (500) watts until caramel dissolves.

Moor in His Shirt

Sophisticated

380 calories per serving
Preparation time: 20 minutes
Cooking time: 2 (2½) minutes

Serves: 4 people

3 eggs, separated	
3 tbs. sugar	
2 oz. plain chocolate	
⅓ cup instant chocolate powder, sweetened	
2 tbs. ground hazelnuts	
1 tbs. rum	
Pinch salt	
2 tbs. butter	
⅓ cup pouring cream	

Beat egg yolks and sugar to a thick, fluffy white cream. • Grate chocolate or chop finely. Mix into egg cream, together with chocolate powder, hazelnuts and rum. Beat egg whites with salt till stiff, then fold into mixture. • Butter 4 individual soufflé dishes and fill three-quarters full with mixture. Cook for 2 (2½) minutes at 600 (500) watts. • Allow to cool slightly, turn out, then turn over again and put onto plates. Pour cream around base while still warm and serve at once.

Variations: These little shapes can additionally be coated with melted chocolate and decorated with whipped cream. Break 2 oz. plain chocolate into pieces for coating and warm for 20 seconds at 600 (500) watts. Around Christmas, a nice touch is the addition of 1 tsp. gingerbread spices, and the substitution of a light vanilla sauce or a warm wine cream (recipe page 114) for the cream.

Lemon Cheese Slices

Easy to prepare

260 calories per serving
Preparation time: 15 minutes
Cooking time: 7½ (8) minutes

Serves: 4 people

2 large egg yolks	
1 tbs. sugar	
1 small organically grown orange	
1½ tbs. flour	
3 egg whites	
Pinch salt	
1 tsp. butter	
For the filling:	
2 large egg yolks	
Juice of 1 lemon	
2½ tbs. sugar	
2 tsp. gelatine	
1 cup full cream curd cheese	
1 tbs. white wine	
¼ cup raspberries or blackcurrants	

Whisk egg yolks and sugar to a thick cream. Wash orange in hot water before grating rind. Squeeze orange, then mix into cream with grated rind. Stir in flour. Beat egg whites and salt till stiff and fold in. • Butter a shallow rectangular pan, spoon in mixture and cook for 4 minutes at 490 (500) watts. • Turn out cake. • To make the filling, cook egg yolks with lemon juice and 1 tbs. of the sugar for 2½ (2¾) minutes at 360 (330) watts. Turn every 30 seconds. • Soak the gelatine in cold water. Stir curd cheese and remaining sugar into the egg cream. • Warm wine for 1 (1¼) minute at 600 (500) watts. Dissolve gelatine in it. • Wash berries, then stir into egg cream with wine-gelatine mix. • Put one half of cake into loaf pan. Spoon in filling and cover with other half cake. • Chill for 2 hours.

Blackberry Roll

Easy to prepare, economical

330 calories per serving
Preparation time: 20 minutes
Cooking time: 6 (6:½) minutes

Serves: 4 people

1 tbs. melted butter
1 cup sugar
3 eggs
1 tsp. grated lemon rind
¼ cup flour
¼ cup full cream curd cheese
¼ cup blackberry jam
2 tbs. sugar for sprinkling on dish
2 tbs. powdered sugar

Butter a fairly large browning dish and sprinkle 2 tbs. of the sugar over bottom and sides. • Whisk eggs with remaining sugar and lemon rind till light and foamy. Stir flour into egg mixture. • Pour into browning dish and smooth top. • Bake for 6 (6½) minutes at 600 (500) watts. • Combine curd cheese with blackberry jam. • Sprinkle 2 tbs. sugar over a cloth. Turn cake out onto it, making sure that the pale side is on top. Flatten cake slightly and spread with blackberry mixture. Roll cake up while still warm. • Dust cake roll with powdered sugar and slice before serving.

Tip: Other kinds of jam may be used for the filling, or a thick chocolate or caramel sauce can be used. The cake is baked in a browning dish so that it takes on some color.

Hot Chocolate

Easy to prepare

310 calories per serving
Preparation time: 5 minutes
Cooking time: 7 (7½) minutes

Serves: 4 people

3½ oz. plain chocolate
6 tbs. cream
1 cup generous milk
1 tbs. sugar

Break chocolate in pieces, add cream and about 6 tbs. of the milk into a bowl. Cover and heat for 2 (2½) minutes at 600 (500) watts, till chocolate melts. • Stir thoroughly, then add remaining milk and sugar. Cover and heat again for 5 minutes at 490 (500) watts.

Honey Milk

Good for colds

170 calories per serving
Cooking time: 7 (7¾) minutes

Serves: 4 people

2½ cups milk
¼ cup honey
1 tbs. full cream curd cheese
1 tsp. freshly chopped mint leaves

Mix milk with honey and curd cheese in a bowl. Cover and heat for 2 (2½) minutes at 600 (500) watts. • Stir thoroughly, then add mint, cover and heat again for 5 (5¼) minutes at 360 (330) watts. Pour into heated glasses.

Irish Coffee

Sophisticated

85 calories per serving
Preparation time: 10 minutes
Cooking time: 2 minutes

Serves: 2 people

2 tbs. whipping cream
¾ cup coffee
3 tbs. raw sugar
2 tbs. Irish Whiskey
Instant Chocolate (optional)

Whip cream very lightly, so that it still pours. • Heat coffee with sugar, covered, for 2 minutes at 490 (500) watts. • Pour whiskey into tall glasses or large cups and add coffee till three-quarters full. Pour cream over back of spoon into coffee, and sprinkle with chocolate if desired.

Soothing Tea

Easy to prepare

180 calories per serving
Cooking time: 9 (9½) minutes

Serves: 4 people

4 cups water
1 teabag
¼ cup freshly chopped mixed herbs (chervil, thyme, lemon balm, mint, sage)
⅓ cup sugar
4 slices orange
2 cloves
2 juniper berries

Cover water and heat for 5 (5½) minutes at 600 (500) watts. Add teabag, herbs, sugar and spices to it. • Cover again and heat 4 minutes more at 490 (500) watts. Pour through a strainer into glasses or cups.

Spiced Punch

Easy to prepare

190 calories per serving
Cooking time: 7 (7¾) minutes

Serves: 2 people

⅓ cup red wine
¼ cup sugar
½ tsp. grated orange rind
Juice of 1 orange
1 clove
1 tbs. rum

Put red wine with sugar, orange rind, orange juice and clove into glass punchbowl or jug. • Cover and heat for 2 (2½) minutes at 600 (500) watts. Then allow to draw for 5 (5½) minutes at 360 (330) watts. Add rum.

Tip: To avoid cracking glasses, put a silver spoon into glass and pour punch in slowly.

Driver's Punch

Very quick

170 calories per serving
Cooking time: 2 (2½) minutes

Serves: 2 people

2 cups water
½ cup grape juice
Juice of ½ orange
Pinch cinnamon
3 tbs. sugar
Rum flavoring (optional)
2 slices lemon or orange

Mix all ingredients except lemon or orange slices in a bowl, cover and heat for 2 (2½) minutes at 600 (500) watts. Pour into tall glasses. Cut citrus slices from edge to center and place on rim of glasses.

Apple Punch

Easy to prepare

170 calories per serving
Cooking time: 7 (7¾) minutes

Serves: 2 people

⅓ cup white wine
2 tbs. sugar
½ tsp. grated lemon rind
⅓ cup apple juice
2 cloves
1 tbs. Calvados

Mix white wine in bowl with sugar, lemon rind, apple juice and cloves, then cover and heat for 2 (2½) minutes at 600 (500) watts. Stir thoroughly, cover again and allow to stand for 5 (5¼) minutes at 360 (330) watts. Add Calvados if so desired, and strain into glasses.

Mulled Wine

Rather more expensive

190 calories per serving
Cooking time: 8 (8¾) minutes

Serves: 4 people

2 cups red wine
4 cloves
1 bay leaf
2 sticks cinnamon
1 cup sugar
4 orange segments
1 lemon, sliced

Mix all ingredients in a bowl, cover and heat for 3 (3½) minutes at 600 (500) watts. Then allow to stand for 5 (5¼) minutes at 360 (330) watts. Strain into glasses.

Index